Many Parts Towards the Whole

Rosie,

With fond memories.

My love,

Ros

Totnes resident

Many Parts Towards the Whole

A Journey of Self Transformation

Roslyn Langdon

British Library Cataloguing in Publication Data
A catalogue record for this book is available from the British
Library

Published by Garuda Press
Typeset by CentreHouse Press | inquiries@centrehousepress.co.uk

Author portrait back cover, and Jack and Boris portrait
on page 264 courtesy Paul Roylance

ISBN 978-0-9932961-0-9

Printed and bound by Lightning Source

Acknowledgements

I want to thank my dear friend from childhood, Marg Clouts, for her patient editing and persistent encouragement to "get on with it", also for the helpful comments from my daughter Melanie, Barbara Bridger and Liz Nussbaum. Grateful thanks also to Peter Cowlam, for his help with book production, and Ingrid Benning for the cover image. I want also to acknowledge the special teachers I have been fortunate to meet who have influenced my life. They are Norah Taylor, Penny Nield Smith, BKS Iyengar, William Swartley, David Boadella, Suprapto, Helen Poyner, Venerable Namgyal Rinpoche, Tarchin Hern, Sonam Gyatso, Sensei Doug Duncan, Christopher Titmus, Rob Preece, Martine and Stephen Batchelor, and more recent meditation teachers Christina Feldman and John Peacock.

All the world's a stage,
And all the men and women merely players:
They have their exits and their entrances;
And one man in his time plays many parts…

As You Like It, II, VII

To Norah Taylor, who nurtured my potential.

The author, aged eighteen (publicity photo), 1947

CONTENTS

PART ONE 1947–1959

THE ACTRESS

Ambition

Have arrived	3
First job, first love	11
France	24
Marriage	27
South Africa	33
Italy	37
Paris	39
Motherhood	43
Tragedy	51
South Africa (again)	53

PART TWO 1960–1969

THE PEACE ACTIVIST AND DRAMA TEACHER

Surviving in London

Work and relationships	65
A new beginning, another ending	79
The accident	84
Keeping busy	91

PART THREE 1970–1979

THE MEDITATION STUDENT AND YOGA TEACHER

Spiritual Awakening

Teaching   99
Namgyal Rinpoche   107
Canada   111
Mexico   116
Crete and Samos   122
Living in Gloucestershire   126
Primal Integration   132
India   138
Search for a centre   146

PART FOUR 1980–1989

THE THERAPIST

Inner and Outer Exploration

Holland   155
Journey to South America   161
Peru   166
Further psychotherapy training   171
Return to South Africa   175
Move to Somerset   180
Round-the-world trip, USA   193
Hawaii   201
Japan   203
Malaysia and Thailand   206
Totnes   209

PART FIVE 1990–1999

THE WORKSHOP FACILITATOR AND TRAINER

Achievement

Personal growth and training workshops	217
Russia	220
Return to Russia	227
South Africa	232
Movement and meditation	238

PART SIX 2000–2010

THE WRITER AND ETERNAL STUDENT

Towards Freedom

Death of the Rinpoche	245
Canada	249
New Zealand	251
Conclusion	258

PART ONE
1947–1959

The Actress
Ambition

Have Arrived

As the boat docked at Southampton that August morning in 1947, I knew I had at last come home. I was now eighteen, already an actress of some experience, and bursting with ambition. I was armed with a bunch of letters of introductions to several influential people and ready to enter the great British Theatre! After two weeks aboard the *Durban Castle*, a Union Castle Line ship plying between Cape Town and Southampton after the war, I couldn't wait to set foot on "England's green and pleasant land". Yet I was puzzled to discover that the fields seen from the train taking me and my mother to London were the colour of my native veld. This was the end of the hot dry summer of 1947.

At the tender age of four I had made the decision to be an actress when I grew up, after experiencing an audience applauding my playing the Sleeping Beauty in a kindergarten play. As I pricked my finger and collapsed to the floor, I got the giggles, and the audience laughed with me. Later, aged eight, appearing as Marigold, the little girl who dreams up the story of Toad and his riverbank friends in *The Wind in the Willows* at the

Library Theatre, Johannesburg, I was completely hooked. I left school at sixteen, and began to get parts in radio plays for the South African Broadcasting Corporation, and then in four theatre productions touring South Africa's largest cities.

At Waterloo Station we found a taxi and gave the driver the address of a boarding house where several South African theatre friends had stayed. What followed was a sightseeing tour with famous landmarks pointed out on the way – Buckingham Palace, Hyde Park Corner, through Hyde Park to Marble Arch, past Regent's Park, St John's Wood, up the Finchley Road to Frognal, finally stopping at number 26, one of an identical row of tall red-bricked Victorian terraced houses. I found it strange to see houses packed so tightly together.

At the boarding house it took me a day or two to get used to sharing a room with my mother, English breakfasts, and the dangerous gas boiler over the bath, which had to be lit with a match in order to obtain hot water. Outside I became aware of London's blackened chimneysweep face and overgrown bombsites – neglected buddleia-covered areas. London at this time was like a tired, grey old lady. However, soon my days were taken up with making appointments to see agents, theatre directors and radio producers, and finding my way around the West End. First I had to prepare for auditions to drama schools. I was disappointed to find that RADA could only offer me a place in their preparatory school for young students, as the main training was reserved for former members of the armed forces. With eighteen months' professional experience of theatre and radio performances in South Africa behind me I dismissed this offer out of hand. The most exciting drama school at that time, the Old Vic School, run by Michel Saint-Denis, could only offer me a place the following year, as their present quota was unfortunately full.

I therefore set up my own training. There were dance classes in ballet, musical comedy, and tap with the legendary Buddy Bradley. Singing lessons were arranged for me with Madame Rosina Buckman, a famous former Australian singer, and I signed up at the City Literary Institute for lectures on the English Romantic movement, the story of theatre and drama, and a course on aesthetics. Evenings were spent in an orgy of theatre-going, buying seats in the gods, where I feasted on a meal of American and English musicals, including Ivor Novello in *Perchance to Dream*, and AP Herbert's *Bless the Bride*. I was thrilled to see Sybil Thorndike and her husband Lewis Casson in *The Linden Tree*, and Emlyn Williams in his own play *Trespass*. A confirmed balletomane, I visited the Royal Opera House in Covent Garden as often as I could. At the Albert Hall I heard a young Yehudi Menuhin, Arthur Rubinstein and Jascha Heifetz from standing room, high up close to the roof. I was like a child in a large available sweetshop!

I was beginning to get auditions at Broadcasting House and Alexandra Palace, then home of television. Sitting in an agent's office one day I was asked to find a stage name. My father, who had a fine dramatic tenor voice, sang under the name of David Langdon; the surname went well with my forename, so I adopted it there and then. A friend I saw a great deal of at that time was Roy Hartstein, who as Roy Hart was to go on to form the Roy Hart Theatre at the Abraxas Club in Hampstead, and to create an international theatre centre in southwest France. Roy had been a fellow-student of my beloved Norah Taylor who had taught us speech and drama at her studios in Johannesburg. I had played Hermia to Roy's Oberon in a production of *A Midsummer Night's Dream*. Later he gave an impressive performance at Wits University as Peer Gynt. In London he began to have singing lessons with Alfred Wolfsohn, who taught a method of singing the full scale of the piano, which Roy developed and later passed on to his theatre students. We spent some happy days on Hampstead Heath that autumn, my first experience of the glory of autumn colours. This was in stark contrast to blackened city buildings and bombsites, which were still evident two years after the war. With my single-minded aim to work in the British theatre, strangely I seemed oblivious to the trials of war the country had suffered and miraculously survived!

Two events stand out during my first few weeks in

London. About ten days after I arrived, while my mother was visiting her uncle in Sunderland, a fellow-resident at the boarding house suggested I might like to accompany him on a business trip to Birmingham. This was a chance to venture out of London for the day. It wasn't long after we set off before his hand began to stray towards my lap, and I started to feel uncomfortable. By the time he stopped the car by some woods with the suggestion that we stretch our legs, I felt decidedly nervous. I tried to keep my distance but he closed in, trying to kiss me. I laughed it off and managed to get back to the car hoping he had got the message that I wasn't interested. Fortunately he did, and for the rest of the journey I endeavoured to act as though nothing untoward had happened. I didn't realise at the time what a potentially dangerous position I had put myself in. The second event occurred a few weeks later. A newspaper reporter arrived at the front door asking to see me. A day or two earlier I had been shocked to read a newspaper report that an actress friend, whom I had last seen at my farewell party in Johannesburg, and whom I was expecting to meet again soon in London, had disappeared off the *Durban Castle* on its next voyage from Cape Town. A steward had answered an alarm call from her cabin late at night. The door was opened by a fellow-steward, James Camb, who reassured him that the bell had been rung by mistake. Later he told a court that while having sex with Gay she had asked him to put his hands round her throat to increase the pleasure. When she collapsed, he panicked, and fearing she was dead, had bundled her body through the cabin porthole. I was naturally shaken by the news, not least because I remembered flirting with James Camb myself on the same boat. I remembered that he was particularly good looking. I was approached as my address was in Gay's address book, but there was little that I could say about her apart from the fact that she was an attractive sophisticated twenty-two-year-old actress. I had known her for only a few months. During the trial more details emerged, and despite the absence of a body, James Camb was sentenced to life imprisonment. A few years ago I read of his release. Sometime after the trial a human hand with rings identified as belonging to Gay was discovered, after a shark was caught and cut open: an extraordinary event if one is to believe it.

I was beginning to learn that in spite of my confidence and youthful exuberance, the world was not the safe place I believed it to be. After my mother returned home to South Africa to my great relief, I moved to a room near old family friends, where I had my meals, and where they could keep an eye on me. My first act of independence was to smoke a cigarette in bed! I had several cigarette holders mainly for show, and I dressed to look like an actress, in high heels that made my feet ache and gave me corns, but they did add to my height, and I wore hat, gloves and shoes to match when visiting agents and attending interviews and auditions.

I began to audition for BBC Radio at Broadcasting House. I had done a good deal of radio work with the South African Broadcasting Corporation in the two preceding years. I had played the part of Little Lord Fauntleroy in a six-weeks' serial version of the book, the life of Fanny Burney the diarist, all of Nora's children in Ibsen's *A Doll's House* with Gwen Ffrangcon-Davies, and again with her in *Mother Courage* playing the almost impossible part in radio, that of her dumb daughter. There was a fine play of Roy Campbell, the poet, about the Spanish Civil War, and the BBC producer Philip Wade's play, *Mild and Bitter*, directed by him, set in the London Blitz. Here in London there were auditions at fringe theatres, and at the Aldwych Theatre, and I was put up for parts in a couple of films, but still no actual engagement. I decided to give myself until 20th January, my birthday, and if I had no work by then I would consider returning home. On the 21st January I had an appointment with Freddie Piffard, who managed several theatres, including the Duke of York's in St Martin's Lane and the Theatre Royal at Richmond. When I attempted to show him my press cuttings from productions in which I had appeared in South Africa, his response was "You colonials are all liars. Why don't you go back where you came from?" Needless to say I left his office in tears. However on arrival at my lodgings I was met with a message to phone his office immediately. Was I interested in playing James Barrie's Mary Rose in

Dundee? I would have gone anywhere to play the part! I had studied the play of the same name, and had used an extract as an audition piece. I immediately sent off photographs and CV, discovering at the same time that Dundee was in Scotland. Meanwhile I carried on with my classes and saw the Christmas productions of *Where the Rainbow Ends* and *Peter Pan* and the fabulous Mae West in her show *Diamond Lil.*

A week later, just when I was beginning to give up hope, there was a phone call from Dundee with some questions, after which I received a telegram confirming the engagement, with the information that a ticket would be awaiting me at King's Cross, and giving the time of an overnight train to get me there for the first rehearsal at 10.30 the following morning. I was ready to travel with my large theatrical skip – a waterproof-lined wicker basket, emblazoned with my initials, and my beloved grease-paint make-up box. My British career was about to take off with a principal part in a foremost repertory theatre company! This was the chance that I had been waiting for!

First Job, First Love

Coming from an affluent background of servants, private swimming pools and tennis courts, and a couple of years when I was involved in an exotic theatrical lifestyle, which included nightclubbing with such well-known figures as the millionaire John Schlesinger, and exiled European royalty in the shape of the young princes Nicholas and Alexander of Yugoslavia and the young King of Romania – after that Dundee was a complete culture shock! I found myself suddenly plunged into a cold, grey puritanical world. This was a world where gas lighting was still used in some houses, and where alcohol was brewed in tenements, using *stairhead gas*. But actors were in a world apart, and I felt at home in the rehearsal room and more than happy to be working again. I was to be attached to the touring company. After three weeks' rehearsal I would find myself touring the play to sixteen small towns for three weeks, including JM Barrie's birthplace, Kirriemuir. We would travel in a theatre bus, arriving at the performance hall a couple of hours before curtain-up in order to set up scenery and lighting, iron costumes and grab a cup of tea.

We couldn't then leave after the show until the set, costumes and props had been struck and loaded on our van. Some of the towns visited were an hour or two's distance away, so sometimes we were not back in our digs until after midnight. When I discovered myself playing the title role again in the next play, with rehearsal all day from 10.30 a.m., I began to learn what hard work was! Although when playing in the touring company we were privileged to have three weeks to rehearse each play, we had to find time to learn lines – usually late at night, after arriving back at our digs, and while travelling in the van. I never found learning lines easy, and first nights were always a test of nerves. There was the constant fear of "drying". Sundays were precious times for catching up on washing clothes, and hair, socialising and relaxing. Sometimes we would watch a dress rehearsal at the main theatre. The director, AR Whatmore, a well-known West End director, had had to leave London for health reasons. He was able to draw some excellent actors to his theatre. When I first arrived I found Richard Todd preparing to go to London for his screen test in *The Hasty Heart*, and later Barbara Jefford and Virginia McKenna joined the company.

After *The Patsy* came *Pygmalion*, *Quiet Weekend*, *An Inspector Calls* and *Pink String and Sealing Wax* in the main theatre. My digs during this time were in a tall grey stone detached house up a hill at the top of town. Our landlady, known as Mrs G, was a pale, pink-eyed bitter little woman with wispy, mousy hair worn in a bun, whose husband had left her for another woman, and was living across the River Tay in Tayside, a fact she had a habit of repeating with vehemence. She had been taking in "theatricals" for years, and a much quoted saying of hers referring to the morals of actors was "The moment the curtain is down they're at it like knives!" She was known to prowl around at night waiting to catch out any unsuspecting couples. There were perhaps half a dozen of us living in her house, each room with its gas fire, where an evening meal would be waiting after the performance. At times the meal was so unpalatable that quite a few fish pies were known to have been flushed down the toilet.

In spite of the grey city, the cold weather and the long hours of work, I was happy. I was leading a life I loved, without restrictions, and I enjoyed the journeys out through the countryside. I was seeing lambs for the first time, and spring flowers. The company was my family and I enjoyed the attention I got from some of the men, particularly the young manager Michael Thompson. I was sometimes teased by my fellow-actors (I was the youngest member of the company) for my dedication to the Stanislavsky method. This was a way of bringing one's own experiences and emotional memories to a character. Not all the actors were as ambitious and single-minded as I was. I must have caused them some irritation with my unfailing fresh enthusiasm, when some of them were worn out with the strain of the war years and with constant touring. On one occasion it was suggested by the director that I play the character as myself, which brought forth a strange heartfelt cry from me, "But I don't know who I am!" I have been on this search ever since!

Initially my wage was four pounds a week. Two pounds went on rent, one pound was for lunches and one pound went into a savings account. From this early training I developed the ability to manage money, always making a little go far. There was no chance of "repairing to the pub" after the show during the week, as they closed at 9 or 9.30. Women weren't allowed in unless accompanied by a male, and then only in the private bar. On Sundays we often had a midday meal at the local hotel, where we were canny enough to sign in at the reception area as visitors to the town, just passing through, in order to be able to buy a drink, as alcohol was unavailable on Sundays except to visitors! My mother wrote weekly letters, signing off with "I hope this finds you as it leaves me likewise." She had been to secretarial college before she married my father, at the age of eighteen. There were also the occasional food parcels from home. Food was still rationed at that time in Britain. What I enjoyed most were the tins of condensed milk. I would puncture a hole and drink straight from the tin.

In London for the summer break, it was back to theatregoing. I got to see a production of *Mary Rose* at the Embassy Theatre in Swiss Cottage one night, and ballet at

Covent Garden the next. Then after a Bristol Old Vic production of *Hamlet* at the St James Theatre, I left the next day for Stratford-on-Avon with a South African friend. We were unable to find accommodation in Stratford and so travelled over each day that week from our hotel in Warwick. In glorious weather we explored Stratford, and Warwick, rowed on the river and visited Leamington Spa. We managed to see *The Winter's Tale*, *Hamlet* with Robert Helpmann, and *Troilus and Cressida* with Paul Scofield, with whom I fell in love. Merilyn and I were young and free, and without a care in the world. As two nineteen-year-olds we lay on top of our beds during the hot nights and talked daringly of being ravished!

Returning to London I took in one more production, *The Glass Menagerie* with the American actress Helen Hayes, before returning to Dundee. I was due to start rehearsals for the leading part in a new Scottish play *The Gowk Storm* the following week, and had arranged to spend my free week with Michael Thompson, the tour manager, with whom I had grown quite close that year. There was a touch of Svengali and Trilby in our relationship. I was pretty, naïve and unworldly, and had much to learn about life. Michael was a serious, quiet-spoken, slight, fair-haired young man, five years my senior. He had started out as an actor at the Newcastle Playhouse near his home, and went on to become Joan Littlewood's first manager of Theatre Workshop after the war, before being asked to set up the touring section of the Dundee Repertory Theatre. It was through Mike that I was a member of the company at all. As a friend of Freddie Piffard, Mike had telephoned him after I had left his office, asking him to suggest an actress to play the leading role of *Mary Rose*, as the Australian actress they had engaged had to return home unexpectedly. Freddie had told him he knew nothing about me but I looked right – small, dark, attractive and vivacious! Mike and I shared digs with several other company members, including the director, AR Whatmore. To my delight Mike took me to Glasgow to meet his friend Hugh MacDiarmid, the renowned Scottish poet, where we had tea at his home together with Valda, his wife of the brilliant red hair. Then off for a dirty weekend at a country inn in St Cyrus where we spent most of the time in bed, not least because of the incessant rain. Soon after we had met we were at a party together where I stood helplessly by as Michael had what I later realised was an angina attack. During the attack he repeated "I am going to die, I am going to die." He was only twenty-four. Later he told me that due to a congenital heart condition, doctors had told him he was unlikely to reach the age of thirty. Another time, while staying with Marie, his theatre director friend in London, he had a further attack during our lovemaking, which I found frightening.

After my success in *The Gowk Storm* we opened the autumn tour with Noël Coward's *Hay Fever* and started rehearsals of Barrie's *Dear Brutus*. We took these plays to

Orkney and the Shetland Islands in October – a week in each place, with another week in Inverness. I loved this time. The company travelled to Aberdeen by train and from there we flew in two chartered biplanes, each holding six passengers, to Shetland. We flew low enough to view the sunken German fleet at Scapa Flow. Our arrival at the airport on the island was delayed while a small flock of sheep was cleared from the only runway. With matinees and run-throughs during the afternoons we were left the mornings for sightseeing, while each night after the show was party time! The Shetlanders had a great tradition of hospitality, and we were treated royally. We left reluctantly for Orkney at the end of the week, after making some good friends, including the crew of a Russian ship moored in the harbour.

Arriving in Orkney we did two performances at Stromness, then moved to the Temperance Hall at Kirkwall. This turned out to be a more sober week as the island was dry at the time. However we were being wonderfully fed. Rationing, although still operating on the mainland, didn't seem to apply to the islands. Next call was a week in Inverness. The unexpected glory of autumn in the Highlands has remained vivid in my memory. There was a memorable bus ride to Fort Augustus, and a visit to Loch Lomond. Then back to Dundee and rehearsals for *Little Women*, and for me, rehearsals for the Player Queen in a production of *Hamlet* the next week in the main theatre. After both these productions came *Arsenic and Old Lace*, which we played on Christmas Day, and on 1st January 1949 we were expected to attend rehearsals for *See How They Run* after an all-night Hogmanay party! This was dedication indeed. For me the theatre at this time was my life, my only reality. I couldn't imagine not being involved in the life of the theatre, whereas the everyday world felt unreal to me.

My former elocution and drama teacher in South Africa, Norah Taylor, who had greatly influenced my life since teaching me at the age of four at kindergarten, arrived in Scotland to visit me, unfortunately catching me in the current production of *Arsenic and Old Lace*, a particularly dull part. If only it could have been the next play, *Thunder Rock*, where I played the part of a nineteenth-century emancipated woman, Melanie Kurtz, one of a group of ghost passengers on a journey by boat to the New World from Europe, conjured up by a twentieth-century lighthouse keeper. In the spring I left the company, took a train to Sunderland to visit my mother's family, then back to London for more auditions at the BBC and theatres round London. During this time I visited the Old Vic for productions of *Antigone*, *The Proposal*, and *The School For Scandal* with Laurence Olivier and Vivien Leigh. I also saw *Adventure Story* with Paul Scofield twice! My greatest experience of all was Elia Kazan's production of Arthur Miller's *Death of a Salesman* with the film actor Paul Muni.

A month later I was on my way to Llandudno with a contract for a summer season with Marie Hopps, who had directed me in some productions at Dundee. After two difficult months without him I was joined by Mike for three weeks in May. This was followed by an uncomfortable ten-day visit from my parents. They appeared so out of place at my bed-and-breakfast lodgings with their South African accents and inappropriate clothes – my father wearing a trilby hat! Soon after I had a more appreciated visit from Howard Goorney of Joan Littlewood's Theatre Workshop Company in Manchester. He was a great friend of Mike's from the time when Mike was general manager of the company. I think he came to look me over, to find out if I met with his approval!

Mike was anxious to get me back into the company at Dundee, and the opportunity came in the most unexpected way. At the end of the six month's season at Llandudno I met up with my old school friend Jo, who took me to her lodgings in London to meet her new husband, and where I spent an uncomfortably embarrassing night sleeping on the floor in the same room together with them. Jo and I had been at Johannesburg Girls' High School together, but we didn't actually meet until taking part in civic celebrations at the Wanderers Stadium, where we found ourselves marching round in time to a brass band. We started a conversation. Although two years older, Jo and I became firm friends through discovering our mutual love of Noël Coward and Ivor Novello's music. I lived up the hill in Mountain View and Jo lived in the valley in Orange Grove. We would then often meet halfway on Sylvia Pass. We spent as much time as we could together reading Noël Coward's plays in each other's homes, and singing the songs nostalgically as sentimental teenagers. I missed Jo terribly when I first came to England, and eagerly awaited her brilliantly written letters, which continued for many, many years.

The next afternoon there was a telephone call from Mike. He was calling from Orkney where the company was on tour with an adaptation of *Wuthering Heights* and Somerset Maugham's *The Circle*. There was an urgency in his voice. "Could you get yourself to King's Cross tonight for the eight o'clock overnight train to Aberdeen? We need you up here to take over by tomorrow night. Norma, playing Isabella in *Wuthering Heights*, has fallen downstairs and broken some ribs. I'll alert the morning plane for Kirkwall to stand by for you. I'll be there to meet you."

Sure enough a ticket was waiting for me at the station, and I was lucky enough to get a sleeper. At Aberdeen the next morning I took a taxi to the airport. There was the plane waiting on the only runway, a small twelve-seat biplane. To make sure it didn't take off without me my taxi driver drove up the runway to meet it nose to nose. It had been held for me, and feeling like a VIP I ran up the steps, while the engine started up before I had even reached my seat.

Meeting me at the airport bus terminal Mike quickly explained that I would go on stage that night, script in hand, and would be expected to learn the part as soon as possible. My first rehearsal was called that morning. I received a less than welcome reception from the cast. Norma was a popular member and they resented my taking her place, notwithstanding the circumstances. They also naturally resented having to rehearse again in their free time. However my job was to master a large, demanding part of Isabella in as short a time as possible. By Thursday night I had the part under my belt, and by the Saturday night I was beginning to enjoy it.

The company had now been in Orkney for two weeks, with the presentation of Somerset Maugham's *The Circle* during the first week, with Peggy Mount playing the lead. Luckily Norma had only a small part in this play, which I put my mind to learning before opening the following week in Inverness. We then returned to Dundee ready for a six-week tour of both plays.

On the first night of the following play, *Fly Away Peter*, arriving back from a weekend visit to his mother in Newcastle, Mike duly presented me with a diamond and sapphire ring. Before I had even taken in the significance of the ring the news had gone out of our engagement, and the local paper appeared with an announcement and photo of us. I wasn't sure if I even wanted to be engaged, but it seemed to please the people around us, so I went along with it. I wasn't in love with Michael at that time, but I valued him as a good friend and mentor. I was being educated in Marxist politics, and literature. I was committed to my career and had always believed I wouldn't think about marriage until I was in my late twenties. The theatre was my life. Everyday life felt unreal to me, and, as I have said, I couldn't imagine ever not being involved in the life of the theatre. I was totally dedicated to it. At the beginning of December we opened with a three-week tour of *The Importance of Being Earnest*, and by the end of December I went home with Mike to meet his mother and close friends.

In spite of my convictions, nine months later we were married. I was twenty-one and could legally marry without parental consent, which I knew I would never receive. After all I was Jewish, and Michael was a flaxen-haired Communist atheist, of Scottish-Irish descent. He would have been even less acceptable only if black!

At the beginning of 1950 I did a tour of provincial repertory theatres, Newcastle, York and Sheffield, for the prospect of future work, before returning to London for interviews. I visited the West End for productions of *Daphnis Laureola* with Edith Evans, *Ring Round the Moon* with Dorothy Tutin and Paul Scofield (I was to wear her lovely ball gown of grey tulle when I played the part the following year), and *A Streetcar Named Desire*. The next month I was back in Llandudno to rehearse the part of a crazy child that I had played there in the thriller *Loophole* the previous summer. We subsequently toured the play in Hastings, Chatham, Bournemouth, Eastbourne, Stoke Newington and Brighton. Afterwards, back in London, I went to see Michael Redgrave in *Venus Observed*. That was the performance where he fainted on stage and the curtain had to be brought down. I believe the play continued with his understudy.

France

In May that year Mike and I took our first holiday together. The British Council arranged a week of theatre visits for him in Paris. We flew from the airport in Croydon on a lovely spring day. Chestnut trees, lining the boulevards, wore their best pink and white blossoms. We had booked to stay in the Hotel Terrass, in the street of the title of the book *The Narrow Street* by Elliot Paul, where as an American he lived during the war. After the war he returned and wrote again of the street, and of the inhabitants who had survived. Being able to stay there felt particularly poignant. That first night we attended a theatre in Montmartre close by. Subsequently we watched *Tartuffe* at the Comédie-Française, *La Prisonnière* with Pierre Blanchard, the Folies Bergère, and on the Sunday a matinee performance of *Cherie* with Jean Marais, and an evening performance of *A Streetcar Named Desire* with the great Arletty. Blanche's famous line "*Voulez-vous coucher avec moi ce soir?*" was here delivered in English. It was the most perfect romantic time – Paris in the spring, Juliette Gréco in black singing in basement venues, Jean-Paul Sartre holding court with his fellow-

Existentialists! Here we were, young and in love, exploring the city and indulging in its culinary delights. On this my first visit to France I enjoyed trying out my school French, hit or miss as it was. Mike, always looking debonair as a theatre manager, with his bowtie and smoking a pipe (he used a tobacco called Baby's Bottom, which smelled so sweet), now appearing more relaxed in casual clothes.

At the end of that week we took a train to the Riviera and got off at Cagnes-sur-Mer. Leaving our luggage at the station we climbed the hill to the village of Cagnes in the hot afternoon sun and slept till the evening in our *pension*. We spent the next week in this delightful ancient village becoming acquainted with the surrounding countryside. On one occasion we walked through fields of cultivated flowers being grown for the perfume industry, to St Paul, and on to Vence, where to our surprise we discovered Gordon Craig's house. Craig was the brilliant theatre designer, son of the great actress Ellen Terry. Unfortunately it wasn't possible to meet him. On our return to Paris and the hotel, I was presented with my unworn nightdress found under my pillow the previous week! After the Louvre there was a final visit to a theatre, the ballet *Carmen* with Roland Petit and Moira Shearer.

The day after arriving home I auditioned for Graham Greene's "The Living Room "at the Globe Theatre that morning and for "Off the Record" at the Richmond Theatre that afternoon.

The next night we saw the great Donald Wolfit at the Bedford Theatre in Camden Town in the Victorian melodrama *The Silver King*. Then after an intense week of interviews, I found myself rehearsing and playing in a production called *The Red Light* in Loughborough!

In June, Mike moved into a room in Gordon Sanderson's home in Hampstead. Gordon was General Secretary of Actors' Equity, where Michael was now employed as civic theatre organiser. The government had recently recommended that local councils should spend one penny in the pound to establish local civic theatres, and Mike was currently touring the country, meeting local councillors and acquainting them with what was required. Meanwhile I returned to see the Donald Wolfit Company in a performance of the melodrama *The Bells*, to Drury Lane to see the musical *Carousel*, Alec Guinness in TS Eliot's *The Cocktail Party* and the musical *Brigadoon*.

That summer I started rehearsals for two plays with the Canterbury Players. This was historically an amateur company that came together with productions during Canterbury Cricket Week each summer, and whose policy was to employ professionals for the leading parts. This gave me the opportunity, at the age of twenty-one, to play Lady Teazle in Sheridan's *The School for Scandal*. It was here I learned the importance of cricket in English upper-class society and where who and what one's father was, was of the utmost importance!

Marriage

August was taken up with auditions, singing lessons and interviews with Colchester and Ipswich Repertory Theatres. I started to look for and found a tiny mews flat in Kinnerton Street, Knightsbridge, where several famous people in the theatre already lived. Mike's mother had had a fatal accident in July, and we had gone up to Newcastle for the funeral. With no home now to return to he felt the urgent need for us to set up a home together, and thus a good reason to get married. Once again I found myself going along with the situation. So on the morning of 1st September I went shopping with old friend Jo. As I was joining the Ipswich Arts Theatre for their next season I had a read-through of the first play that afternoon. The next morning Jo and I took a taxi to Hampstead Register Office in time for my wedding to Michael Thompson. I was twenty-one and he twenty-six. A few friends accompanied us back to my old flat off the Finchley Road for drinks before we left for a one-night honeymoon at the Complete Angler pub in Marlow. The following day I started rehearsals for *Little Lambs Eat Ivy*. After a week of rehearsals in London the cast left for

Ipswich, where I had to find digs. After another week of rehearsals the play opened and rehearsals began for *The Heiress*, followed by the title role in *Claudia*. For the rest of the season Mike and I met each weekend alternately in Ipswich and London. There was one memorable Friday night when I found him waiting in my room in an uncharacteristic fury after I had thoughtlessly accepted an invitation for a drink at the local pub from an actor who rather fancied me. He had walked me back to my digs where he left me after an enthusiastic goodnight kiss! I was greeted with "Where the fuck have you been," to which I answered lamely "To the pub." I had no excuse. He had made the journey to be with me after a heavy week's work, and I had treated him with scant regard. This was our first row. Unfortunately every word could be heard by the good churchgoing family in the living-room below, and soon there was a knock on the door and the wife, called Pussy by her family (much to the amusement of my newly-wed self), was ordering me to pack my bags and leave by the next day. As the following day was Saturday with a matinee and evening performance, I was allowed to stay on till the Sunday.

At the end of the Ipswich Theatre season I began a season at the Colchester Rep, opening with a delightful production of *The Rivals*, which was memorable for having the extremely good-looking stage and film star Terence Morgan, in the male role. He would wrap his cloak around me as we waited in the wings to go onstage, while I fantasised about spending a night with him! One evening, while appearing in *A Lady Mislaid*, I set out for the theatre on a bicycle left me by a former cast member at my digs. I was neither confident nor competent on the machine, as I had never been allowed to have one as a child, and on turning right into the main road I was suddenly faced with a motorcycle bearing down on me. The next thing I knew I was flying through the air and landing painfully at the side of the road. Taken to hospital, I protested loudly that I had to be at the theatre within the hour. The motorcyclist hadn't seen me with the setting sun in his eyes, and was knocked unconscious. Meanwhile I was patched up, leg bandaged, arm in a sling, cuts and bruises cleaned, and after an anti-tetanus injection sent off in an ambulance to the theatre, where the curtain had been held for me. I was greeted with applause on my entrance, and with grazed face and limping I got through my part. After all, the show must go on! Mike had a shock on meeting me at Liverpool Station that weekend as the bruises had come out by then.

In the summer I left Colchester to start rehearsals for a musical version of *She Stoops to Conquer*, in which I had a couple of solos to sing. The production opened at Cambridge, where during the week I learned to play darts at the Eagle pub, after scoring a bull's eye with my first dart, and sending my second aim into my foot! I spent a very happy week with days free to punt down the river to Grantchester, remembering my favourite poet, and generally having a romantic time with the same entertaining actor who had got me into so much trouble in Ipswich. After a special performance at the King's Lynn Festival, attended by the then Queen (later the Queen Mother), we were presented to her, while I had difficulty keeping my balance curtseying to her in high heels on cobblestones!

Joining Mike for a holiday in France, we took a train to Saint-Jean-de-Luz near Biarritz. Being the height of the season we had difficulty in finding somewhere to stay, finally landing up in a tiny room in the town, with a hard iron bedstead and stiffly starched cotton sheets. After several days of rain we took advantage of the first sunny day with a walk along the cliff tops. Michael, with his very fair skin, was badly burned, and spent the next few days in bed with a fever. Fed up with the constant rain we took a train across the border into Spain. At Hendaye we found signs of the civil war. As a teenager Michael had campaigned against the civil war and supported the International Brigade. On reaching San Sebastian, we found to our disgust that General Franco and government ministers were holidaying there. We stayed only a couple of days, during which time we visited a bull fight. To my horror and disgust we witnessed eight bulls killed that afternoon. Yet grudgingly I had to admire the colour, the excitement and the theatricality of the scene.

Later that summer, after watching a production of *The Winter's Tale*, with John Gielgud, Flora Robson and

Diana Wynyard, I packed up our London mews home and moved to a flat over a dentist's surgery near the Arts Theatre in Ipswich. Michael was taking over as manager of the theatre, and he felt it would not be wise for me to be part of the company now. So it was back to writing letters, visiting agents and seeking radio work. However I had previously been booked to play one of Beauty's sisters in a Christmas production of *Beauty and the Beast*, directed by Stuart Burge. Michael had invited AR Whatmore to direct his opening 1951 season, and having joined the company at Christmas, Wattie invited me to remain in the company, which I did for the rest of the following year, successfully playing the title role in a musical version of the melodrama *Maria Marten, or The Murder in the Red Barn*, and the Clare Bloom part in *Ring Round the Moon*, where I got to wear the gorgeous grey tulle ball gown she had worn in the recent West End production. We bought a 1936 Singer that year and took trips into the countryside and coastal areas on Sundays. I have memories of picnics in meadows of wild flowers, and the pleasure of the beach at Waldringfield.

By 1953 I was living back in London, initially in Meg Maxwell's flat in Brook Green, while she was touring in France. (Meg had been a member of the Ipswich company.) Sadly she was killed in a car accident there and never returned. I rented a flat in Maida Vale, which when first viewed contained some dubious sado-masochistic artefacts and literature and a strangely disquieting atmosphere. Also on moving in, a full-length mirror crashed to the floor and shattered, filling me with a measure of superstitious dread. I was having further radio and theatre auditions again, including one at the Old Vic. After returning to Ipswich for a revival of *Maria Marten*, I took part in a drama production at the BBC at the weekend and continued at Ipswich in the title role of *Johnny Belinda*, the deaf mute. The following Sunday I was invited to sign the Lord's Prayer at the special service for the deaf at the local church, St Mary-le-Tower, a moving experience.

Later that year I played the French wife in *The Love of Four Colonels* at Guildford. Then back to singing and dancing lessons in London and auditions for the West End productions of Graham Green's *The Living Room*, and Sandy Wilson's *The Boy Friend* at the Players' Theatre. Ten years later Sandy would become a good friend. Then came a television engagement, playing Nell Gwyn in *An Elizabethan Night*. I returned to Ipswich for the Christmas pantomime playing Princess Badroulbadour in *Aladdin*. The company was particularly strong at this time, headed by Paul Eddington and with Val May as director.

South Africa

As there were no more prospects of work on the horizon in 1954, and my parents were urging me to visit them, I decided to take three months off and return to South Africa. Crossing the equator on a Union Castle boat was marked, among other rituals, by a fancy dress ball. Dressed as a Folies Bergère girl I won first prize, presented by the captain. My mother met me at the Cape Town dock, and after a week there visiting friends we took the train for the 1,000-mile journey to Johannesburg. My parents had moved from the large detached house in Mountain View to a small flat in Rosebank. I would have to share a room with my grandfather, who had recently been mugged, and whose bowels had ceased to function due to the shock. Being back in my family's atmosphere, which had always been difficult for me, and having been used to my independence, living here was now not easy. Added to this was the fact that being a woman without a partner in Johannesburg, I was completely dependent on my family and friends to get about.

Fortunately I quickly renewed my contact with radio

and theatre producers with whom I had previously worked, and within a week I was recording for radio, and auditioning once again for the Dorothy Tutin part in *The Living Room*. When then offered the part, I discovered that the staging wasn't for another couple of months, by which time I would be on my way home. Meanwhile I continued to do several radio dramas and a personal radio interview, and managed to lead quite a hectic social life with some old and some new friends.

Before leaving for Venice on a Lloyd Triestino ship, *The Europa*, I spent a week in Durban, where I was fortunate enough to see Danny Kaye arrive on a visit to South Africa. Michael and I planned to have a reunion in Venice, that most romantic of all cities. We had missed each other greatly. I suspect he did more than I, judging from the almost daily letters I received. After all I had managed to have a rather exciting time!

The journey up the east coast of Africa was a great experience. Every couple of days we docked and spent some time at a different port, Beira, Dar es Salaam, Mombasa, Mogadishu, Aden, Port Said. At Dar es Salaam I saw my first Arab dhows with their distinctive sails. At Mogadishu we took on a large number of refugees who crowded the ship for the rest of the journey. At Port Said there were trips to the Pyramids, which I resisted, because of the expense, after the beautiful experience of sailing gently through an eau-de-Nil Suez Canal. During the voyage I had become a little too friendly with a

Portuguese medical student named Luis, who spoke practically no English. On going ashore with him at Port Said, a tradesman whose shop we had entered drew him aside with an offer to buy me, but apparently the offer wasn't good enough as Luis refused. However he did buy a knife with which "to kill your husband", a threat I was forced to take seriously as he had a fiery Latin temperament, and was beginning to express serious protestations of love! Towards the end of the voyage he had tried to steer me into a bathroom and into a bath in order to have his evil way with me. Fortunately I was able to escape in time!

The next day, after a brief stop at Brindisi, we made a dramatic early-morning arrival at Venice, seventeen days after leaving Durban. I woke at about six o'clock to discover Santa Maria della Salute moving slowly past the porthole. From the top bunk, where I had climbed in my nightdress for a better view, and just avoided sitting on a pineapple purchase in my excitement, I watched in wonder at other famous landmarks moving past in the early morning mist as we sailed up the Grand Canal. It all felt quite unreal, like watching a film. Now I rushed to get dressed and finish my packing in a fever of excitement at the prospect of meeting Michael again. This was mixed with some apprehension at getting him away before Luis could reach him. The ship had already docked by the time I had climbed on deck with my luggage. On the dockside was a worried-looking Mike, until my frantic waving changed his expression to one of relief. As we finally met, I allowed him only a brief embrace before bundling him off the quayside and away from a potentially dangerous Portuguese. Michael guided me towards the hotel he had booked into the night before, while he related the story of his adventure since getting to the docks that morning. He had arrived by train from London the day before, and gone to bed early in preparation for an early start that morning. On trying to leave the hotel, however, he found the front door locked and no way of opening it. With no one around to help, in desperation he was forced to climb through a downstairs window overlooking a canal, edging himself along a ledge towards the entrance, endeavouring not to slip into the muddy waters lapping against the hotel walls, while desperate to reach the docks in time to welcome me.

Italy

We spent seven idyllic days in Venice. We listened to music in St Mark's Square, and one night there was a concert of sacred music relayed from the Basilica conducted by Leopold Stokowski. We watched glass-blowing on the island of Murano, and I still possess a comic little opaque vase I bought at the time. We spent time at the Gallerie dell'Accademia and marvelled at the magnificent Tintorettos. I was completely blown by his expertise, also the paintings of Veronese. Of La Fenice, I noted in my diary it was the most beautiful theatre in the world. Tragically it was recently burned down in a fire, although later restored. We made a day trip to Vicenza to visit the Palladian Teatro Olimpico built in 1580. This open-air theatre with its stone statues and columns is like no other. Luckily, the day before we left we were able to visit the twenty-seventh Biennale exhibition of contemporary art. What a romantic and rich cultural experience Venice proved to be.

On leaving, we took a train to Rome and spent time visiting all its famous landmarks. At the Vatican City, I was able to view with wonder Michelangelo's Sistine

Chapel mural lying on the floor, unlike my visit more than fifty years later when I viewed it standing crammed into that same space with at least a couple of hundred other tourists. One night we had dinner with Signor Torraca, representative of the International Theatre Institute at the Institute Club. We visited the Eliseo Theatre where we saw a production of *La Bohème* and *Rigoletto*. We visited the Caracalla Baths, a Roman amphitheatre where I stood on the giant stage and spouted a speech from Bernard Shaw's *St Joan*.

From Rome on to Naples and the beautiful island of Capri, taking the funicular up to the town. I was thrilled to be able to visit Axel Munthe's house in Anacapri. I had recently read the famous doctor's book *The Story of San Michele*. Two days later we left for Sorrento and Pompeii. Then back to Naples for a train to Rome, where we visited Raphael's tomb and a magnificent performance of *Turandot* at the Caracalla Baths.

Paris

After a twenty-four-hour train journey we reached Paris, where we visited the Louvre, and saw a memorable exhibition of Impressionist paintings from the USSR at the Maison de la Pensée Française, never before seen in the West. Thereby hangs a tale! This was the first occasion on which the pictures had been allowed out of the Soviet Union. The exhibition was planned to last through the summer. However, the day after our visit, the exhibition was suddenly closed, the pictures removed and hastily returned to Moscow. Rumour had it that a group of White Russians living in Paris since the Revolution plotted to seize back their rightful possessions confiscated at the time of the Revolution. We were extremely fortunate to have been able to view these priceless works, not exhibited again for another thirty years. Before leaving I purchased a Picasso print of *Harlequin and his Companion*, which I still have framed and hanging on my living-room wall, the original of which I was thrilled to find in the Pushkin Museum in Moscow forty years later. On seeing it I couldn't help jumping up and down with joy!

The next exciting event in Paris was a visit to the Sarah Bernhardt Theatre for the first appearance of Berthold Brecht's Berliner Ensemble in *Mother Courage*, with Helene Weigel, Brecht's wife, in the title role. Ken Tynan was also at that performance and wrote an article in his role as *The Observer* drama critic, extolling the importance of Brecht's Theatre of Alienation. (I had met Ken Tynan during my first year in London, when he was just down from Oxford. We had lunch at Vega, the city's first vegetarian restaurant, in Leicester Square, together with a South African friend and her fiancé, who brought him along.) I found it exciting and at the same time bewildering to view the production with the stage lighting full up, glaring white throughout. The next day we returned to England. All of this travelling was before the rise of tourism. We met no other foreigners like us on the way.

Back to a round of auditions, theatre visits and time spent travelling to Ipswich to be with Michael. After a visit to Colchester to meet the producer at the repertory theatre there, run by Bob Digby, a large genial likeable man, I started rehearsals for *Smiling Through*. The day before I had been to the Middlesex Hospital where I discovered I was pregnant. I must have conceived in Venice during those first heady days there! This was an unexpected shock, but I accepted the news on experiencing Michael's obvious delight. After *Smiling Through* came *Family Relations*. My entrance, as a twelve-year-old, was made by jumping onto the stage from a high wall. Six days later, back in our London flat, I was rushed to hospital in an ambulance after haemorrhaging through the night (so much blood!) with a miscarriage, spending the next eight days there. It was a painful, frightening and lonely experience, but it wasn't a planned baby, so I wasn't tremendously disappointed. As soon as I was home it was back to visiting theatres – Margot Fonteyn in *The Bluebird* and *Les Sylphides* at Covent Garden, and the great Gigli at the Albert Hall. Then off to interviews at Boreham Wood film studios, and Lime Grove Television Centre, and auditions at Her Majesty Theatre, Richmond, and Leatherhead Theatres, and the Stoll Theatre for *Toad of Toad Hall*. By December I was rehearsing for *The Three Musketeers* at the Television Centre one day while attending my first rehearsal for the Christmas pantomime, *Cinderella*, at Ipswich. The following week I found myself rehearsing and transmitting live on TV on the Tuesday and Wednesday, and rehearsing at the Ipswich Theatre the rest of the week, playing the fairy queen. The cast there consisted of Clive Revill, who later went on to make films in Hollywood, Elvi Hale, Nick Selby, destined for the Royal Shakespeare Company, Wendy Craig and Paul Eddington, both going on to TV fame. By this time I was pregnant again and experiencing serious morning and evening sickness, with slight bleeding that threatened a further miscarriage. This time I was determined to keep the baby, and spent my time, when not on stage, stretched out on a chaise longue.

At five months, at a performance in the Winter Garden Theatre, the baby was proving to be a dancer while keeping time to the music of some Bulgarian dancers, leaving me exhausted. By now Michael had left his position as general manager at the Ipswich Theatre, and had joined Oscar Lowenstein and Wolf Mankowitz's management as their general manager, and during June 1955 I watched rehearsals of Orson Welles directing and playing the role of Captain Ahab in his own adaptation of *Moby Dick*. Michael found working with him an extraordinary experience. He treated the world as his oyster. However impossible, if there was something he wanted for his production, he had to have it even if it meant sending to the other side of the world for it. At that time he was married to Paola, an Italian princess. She too was expecting a baby, and there were occasions when we met and compared notes. The first night at the Duke of York's Theatre was a great success, with Joan Plowright, later to become Lady Laurence Olivier, the only woman in the cast, playing a cabin boy. After the show, at a party on stage, the great man asked my opinion as to how the show had gone, as he had been used to asking me to watch during rehearsals while he was playing the part of Ahab.

Motherhood

Early that August my mother arrived from Johannesburg to be with me for the birth. Luckily the weather was fine and we took trips down the river to Kew, and to Regent's Park. When the baby finally arrived three weeks late, Michael had to leave the following day to tour with *The Punch Review* for the next few weeks. That meant I was treated as a single parent during my nine days' stay in hospital, in those days seen as a shameful state! I named my daughter Melanie after the character I admired in the play *Thunder Rock*. During the following days at home I wept a good deal alone with a helpless baby and my just-as-helpless mother, used to servants to look after her, and longed for Michael's return. Later, when *The Punch Review* opened in the West End I was able to attend the first night, and the champagne party afterwards. The same week I joined Michael at the Park Lane Hotel for Wendy Craig's wedding party. As I was breast-feeding Melanie I needed to leave the party early. A well-known impresario offered to take me home, and on arrival at the entrance to my flat he attempted to kiss me. By now the milk from my enlarged breasts was dribbling down my blouse. Somehow I managed to tear myself from his grasp and rush upstairs to feed my hungry baby.

Early the following year Sam Wanamaker's production of *The Threepenny Opera* opened at the Royal Court Theatre with Bill Owen as Macheath (Mack the Knife). Michael was the general manager of the production. Later it moved to the Comedy Theatre, and when a member of the cast dropped out I took over the part of a drummer boy, appearing with the folksinger Ewan MacColl at the start of each new scene. For several days I practised drumming with two spoons on a table top. In addition I played one of the prostitutes visited by Macheath, and understudied the part of Polly Peachum. It was a lot to take on, but I loved Kurt Weill's music, and being back on stage again in such a prestigious production was worth it. There were two exciting theatre events that year, the first visit to London of the Berliner Ensemble with *Trumpets and Drums*, and the Bolshoi Ballet, with a performance of *Romeo and Juliet* with the great dancer Galina Ulanova. Her Juliet was breathtakingly moving. At the age of forty she looked a convincing sixteen, and gave a performance I shall never forget. I accompanied Michael to a reception for the ballet company at the Soviet Embassy, where during the evening I was thrilled to find myself sharing a mirror with Ulanova in the ladies' cloakroom!

A memorable event that year was the arrival of Arthur

Miller and his wife Marilyn Monroe for his play *View From the Bridge* at the Comedy Theatre, and her film role with Laurence Olivier in *The Prince and the Showgirl*. As general manager of the Comedy Theatre at that time Michael found himself having to take care of Marilyn when her husband was involved with rehearsals. One time he came home grumbling that he had had Marilyn in his office all day interrupting his work, even having to go out to buy sandwiches for her! At the first night we were seated in the stalls next to Laurence Olivier and his wife Vivien Leigh and with Arthur Miller, awaiting Marilyn's arrival. Just before curtain-up she made an impressive entrance shimmying down the aisle in a wine-red velvet dress moulded to her curves and flaring out from the ankles like a mermaid.

During this time some liberal American artists, including scriptwriters, film actors and directors were beginning to arrive in London to avoid the anti-Communist witch-hunt tribunals set up by Senator McCarthy. As a Communist, Michael was in touch with several of them, and soon we were being invited to meet them. We spent one lovely summer afternoon at the Hampstead home of famous scriptwriters Donald and Ella Ogden Stewart, where Melanie played in their garden with Oona and Charlie Chaplin's children. Another regular visitor there was Katharine Hepburn, and the Greek film actor George Coulouris, who subsequently became a good friend.

In 1957 method acting arrived in London in the form of classes at the London Studio. These weekly classes were run by actors David de Keyser and the American Al Mulak for experienced actors. I had been an enthusiastic follower of the Stanislavsky method after reading his *An Actor Prepares* and *Building a Character*, and had always tried as an actress to put his methods into practice. Here was an opportunity to explore these methods with other dedicated actors. We also explored some of our own life experiences, to open up to the genuine feelings that we could use for the characters in the pieces we prepared to present to the group. In one of these pieces I was partnered by a tall young Scot named Sean Connery. A highlight that year was meeting Tennessee Williams backstage after a first night performance of his play *Camino Real*.

In July, Warren Jenkins, for whom I had worked at Ipswich, asked me to join the cast of *Oh My Papa*, with Rachel Roberts and Peter O'Toole, due for the West End after playing at Bristol Old Vic. There would be a fortnight playing at Brighton's Theatre Royal before coming to the Garrick Theatre. The time coincided with Michael's holiday leave, and I had booked our first holiday with our daughter at Bognor Regis. However another opportunity to appear in the West End won the day, a disastrous decision as it turned out. Once again I joined a cast already played in, and found myself quickly having to learn some intricate steps as a ballerina in a circus scene, and as the back end of a pony! The dress rehearsal at Brighton was a nightmare. Peter O'Toole swore at the management and threatened to leave the show, while I, encased in the pony costume, found it impossible to co-ordinate my steps with those of the front legs. I was sacked on the spot, but had to continue to work out my fortnight's notice while a substitute was found. In addition to the humiliation, I missed Melanie terribly and spent days weeping. After the first week Michael brought her down to join me, as with his holiday leave over he had to return to work. I can still hear her cry of "Mummy" as she ran towards me down the backstage corridor. After another painful week there was a memorable return journey to London in the back of a taxi with Peter's arm around my shoulder singing every Irish song he knew.

February 1957 saw the historic meeting at Westminster Hall for the banning of nuclear testing. On the platform were scientist Linus Pauling, author JB Priestley and politician Aneurin Bevan. I was personally concerned at learning of the likelihood of strontium 90 passing into the milk we drink, and the effect on children. After the meeting a group of us representing the theatre, including the theatre critic Ken Tynan and his then wife Elaine Dundy, marched off to Downing Street to protest, and were met by mounted police wielding batons. I found myself crushed up against the railings opposite Number 10 protecting my head from blows.

Later that year I was asked by Paul Eddington's wife, Trish, to join a group of 500 Quaker women on a march from Marble Arch to Trafalgar Square. In heavy rain I pushed my three-year-old daughter in her pushchair up Oxford Street on the way to Trafalgar Square. This was the historic forerunner of the Easter CND marches, to ban the nuclear bomb, which continued at least for the next twenty or thirty years, and I took part in many of them through the next few years. Apart from my passion for the theatre I had always felt strongly about the need for peace, for the righting of injustice and inequality. I had grown up with it in South Africa, and the inhumanity I witnessed there was a deciding factor in leaving my homeland.

That summer we finally had our first holiday with Melanie. We took a boat across the Channel to Brittany, staying in the Hôtel d'Angleterre at St Cast, high up overlooking the sea. We spent each day on the beach, whatever the weather. That was where Michael discovered calvados! On our return to London we were fortunate enough to hear Paul Robeson sing with that magnificent voice at the Albert Hall.

After our holiday Michael was invited to set up TWW, Television Wales and the West, one of the new independent television companies springing up at that time. His office was based in London but he made frequent visits to the studios in Bristol and Cardiff. Michael was highly thought of in the theatre world as a successful innovator of new theatre projects, from Joan Littlewood's Theatre Workshop, to setting up the Dundee Touring Company, to turning around a dire financial situation at the Ipswich Repertory Theatre, to becoming the general manager of the Oscar Lewenstein/Wolf Mankowitz West End management, with its productions of *The Punch Review*, *Shalom Aleichem*, *Moby Dick*, *The Threepenny Opera* and *View From the Bridge*. Sadly we saw little of each other living in the flat in Maida Vale. Weekdays he was in his office and evenings at the theatre, or with the current production on tour.

During September of 1958 Michael fell ill with acute bronchitis. After two weeks at home in bed he was admitted to the National Heart Hospital, where he remained for three weeks. Melanie became so disturbed by his absence that I took her to the Tavistock Child Guidance Clinic. She would be fine once he was back home, they said. Although he finally recovered from the bronchitis it left his heart weakened. On returning home, he saw a new doctor, recommended by a South African actress friend, who suggested he have an operation to repair the leaking valve of his heart. So early in January he entered the London Hospital in the East End, where, after three weeks of tests, they finally operated on him – the 29th January, his thirty-fifth birthday. I had given him a birthday card the evening before, on my last visit. Unfortunately I had a cold, and not wanting to infect him at this crucial time I refrained from embracing him, leaving him with a cheery "See you later, alligator." No goodbye kiss!

Tragedy

The 29th January 1959 was a particularly dark, gloomy day. I spent the morning at the launderette, while Melanie was at her nursery school in Beauchamp Lodge. During the afternoon I waited for news, together with Michael's old friend, the theatre director Marie Hopps. She had arrived from Manchester a couple of weeks earlier to stay, together with her partner, George, while Mike was in hospital. Just as I was contemplating ringing the hospital, they rang. "Have you anyone with you?" I was asked. On answering in the affirmative, the voice continued, "I have to tell you that your husband is dead." My immediate reaction was to reply with "You must be joking," to which the voice replied sternly "We never joke about such matters."

That evening I went on automatic pilot going through the usual routine of putting Melanie to bed. She had taken to sleeping in my room in her father's bed. (We had never been able to afford a double bed.) That evening she was in particular need of reassurance about her father's welfare – was he still with the doctors and nurses and were they looking after him? From that time on it was

Melanie's pain that I found most painful and poignant to bear. I went on to read the obligatory bedtime story and finally got to bed myself. Unable to sleep I got up and wandered into the living room where Marie and George were sitting. "Do you notice something?" Marie asked. The clock Michael had been presented with on leaving the Ipswich Theatre was ticking away again. It was an eight-day clock and only responded, as I subsequently found out, to his winding practice. "Don't worry, I'll get it going again when I return," he had assured me during both hospital stays. "Did you manage to start it up?" I asked Marie. "No, I haven't touched it," she replied. "It will be Michael returning to keep his promise."

The next few days went by in a blur of making funeral arrangements and contacting friends and Michael's colleagues. I couldn't take in the fact that I had lost forever my best friend, and apart from my father, the only person I felt who had ever loved me. The funeral at Golders Green Crematorium five days later was the first I had ever attended. I didn't know what to expect. I knew that as an atheist Mike would not have wanted a religious address, so we had a period of silence before the coffin, topped with my single wreath of his favourite flowers, anemones, slid relentlessly towards the incinerator, a silence only broken by my despairing cries of "No, no!"

South Africa (again)

The flight to South Africa in March took twenty-five hours, with stops at Rome, Khartoum, Nairobi, Salisbury and finally Johannesburg. I had been persuaded by my parents to come out to South Africa for an extended period, a disastrous decision, as it turned out, not least because I was going from one winter into another, and by the end of that year returning to yet a further winter! We were met by my parents and taken to their small flat in Yeoville. Thus began the worst year of my life. Instead of receiving the love and support that I needed at this time I was subjected to a barrage of resentment and judgement at what I had put them through by marrying out of their faith, and to a man that dies and leaves me practically penniless (£500 in the bank account)! I was too vulnerable to take this treatment for long, and two weeks later we were on a train to Cape Town to join my dearest school friend, Jo. She was holidaying on a lovely beach at Llandudno, on the Cape coast, with her errant then husband Joe, a journalist, and two young sons. Joe had offered to drive us down to Cape Town, but never turned up! So we opted for the two-day train journey. Our stay was short-lived with an atmosphere fraught with domestic strife. I was unhappy enough and Melanie was suffering. How was she to understand, as a three-year-old, what had happened to her father? Later, in an agonising moment, she found her own way. On discovering a dead frog on the road, she asked me what had happened to it, and said "Is this like Daddy?" We moved into a hotel in Sea Point, while I contacted another old school friend in Cape Town. Marge has remained a firm friend to this present day. We stayed on, spending time on the beaches in the autumn sunshine for another few weeks, before reluctantly returning to Johannesburg. The most difficult thing about being there was that I had such a need to talk about Michael, and there was nobody there who knew him. Many a time there, and during the next few years, I continued to grieve, with the lack of sympathetic support. What compounded the grief was my feeling of guilt, that I had not taken the possible consequences of a heart operation seriously enough. There was also guilt about not having reciprocated the deep love that Michael held for me, and the fact that I had not been faithful to it, that I had, in fact, on occasions betrayed his love.

However I needed to earn a living and find somewhere else to live. There followed interviews with some radio producers I had worked with previously. Three weeks later I had my first radio engagement with the South African Broadcasting Corporation, then regular engagements, including the challenge of playing the almost impossible part on radio of the deaf and dumb daughter with Gwen Ffrangcon-Davies in Brecht's *Mother Courage*. Of course I had seen the Berliner Ensemble's production of the play a few years previously. I was interviewed by Springbok Radio about my theatre career in England, followed by some commercial radio work. Meanwhile I managed to rent a rondavel (a traditional round, stone, thatched cottage) on the side of a kopje in the grounds of a sympathetic young writer's house. He and his several black servants kept an eye on us. One day, while walking on the estate, I discovered a cave, blocked by huge boulders. I learned that at a time when Mahatma Gandhi was living in South Africa, he had held meetings at that cave, and to prevent such large numbers of his supporters congregating there, the police had blown up the entrance.

I began a course of typing lessons at the Modern Methods College twice a week, and I set up as a speech and drama teacher from the cottage, with a brass plaque to announce the fact on the wall outside the estate. I also set up a method acting class for actors based on the work I had done at the London Studio. I now found myself teaching actors with whom I had worked as a teenager before leaving for England!

Near the end of that year I discovered to my horror that I was pregnant. I had been going out with a businessman introduced by an old friend, and one night, after several brandies, and completely unprepared, I allowed myself to be seduced. I couldn't possibly have the baby! I was returning to Britain the following month in time for Christmas. The same friend recommended an abortionist, a Scot from Dundee. He arranged to come to the cottage one night, while Melanie, just out of two weeks' quarantine for chickenpox, went to spend the night elsewhere. Apart from being illegal, there was a certain amount of health risk involved. He used a suction method and we talked of his hometown. He suggested I see a doctor afterwards to request a curettage. After haemorrhaging heavily for a week, I was admitted to a medical clinic with what was described as the removal of a polyp. This experience was the last straw in the worst year of my life. There had been some particularly desperate moments, such as walking out into the sea at Llandudno, with little Melanie's terrified cries from the beach of "Mummy, Mummy!" echoing my feelings of despair.

There was also the time at the cottage in Joburg, when I considered ending my misery by putting my head in the gas oven, but I knew I couldn't abandon that little girl. I had to continue living for her sake. Yet I felt so much guilt over Michael's death, having encouraged him to have the operation, without considering the risk involved. What I believed would give him a new lease of life had killed him. I would have to live with this knowledge for the rest of my life. I deeply regret that I never told him I loved him. With an unloving mother, I suspect I was not capable of giving love.

On the 22nd December Melanie and I boarded a Comet plane for London. We ran into a violent storm and were diverted to Entebbe, where we were grounded. Thus in the middle of the night we were taken to a hotel on Lake Victoria, where in the early hours of the morning Melanie insisted on still having her bedtime story. Later that same morning we were on our way again, with stops at Nairobi, Khartoum and Rome. My brother, Theo, two years my senior, having recently graduated from medical school, and who had arrived in England a few years earlier to practise as a psychiatrist, was at the airport to meet us. Now I had to prepare myself to take up life again in England without my beloved partner!

As Isabelle (right) in Christopher Fry's adaptation of Anouilh's *Ring Round the Moon* at Ipswich Arts Theatre, 1952

As Ela (right) in Brandon Thomas's *Charley's Aunt* at Ipswich Arts Theatre, 1952

Doto in *A Phoenix Too Frequent* by Christopher Fry at Ipswich Arts Centre, 1953

Belinda in *Johnny Belinda* by Elmer Blane Harris at Ipswich Arts Centre, 1953

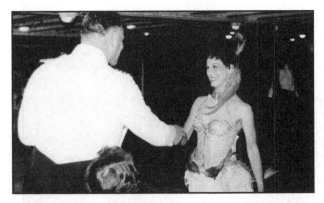

On board ship for Cape Town, receiving congratulations from the captain for winning first prize as a *Folies Bergère* girl in the fancy dress competition, 1953

Author with her mother on Durban beach before boarding a ship for home, 1953

The author, Michael and Melanie in Little Venice park, 1956

PART TWO
1960–1969

The Peace Activist and Drama Teacher

Surviving in London

PART TWO

Work and Relationships

Back in England I now had the task of creating a new life – of finding a way to continue earning a living while caring for my daughter. My nine-month stay in South Africa had lost me the support of some influential theatre people who had offered to help me, including the impresario Oscar Lowenstein and Joan Littlewood, of Theatre Workshop. Now I was on my own and would just have to pick up the pieces and fend for myself. My priorities were clear – I had to find us a home and provide Melanie with the security she needed. The Maida Vale flat was still let, and my lease would soon be up.

"Come and live in Putney," said my friend Joan. A few days later I joined her in the maisonette where she lived with her two sets of twins. The eldest girls were the same age as Melanie. Joan had been an assistant scenic designer at the Ipswich Theatre. She had married the scenic designer, but he had left her when the second lot of twins arrived! She now worked illustrating children's books, including the very popular character of that time Little Joe, and later on Postman Pat, which became a great TV programme. We all mucked in together till I found a room nearby, and then a flat off the High Street. I settled Melanie into the local primary school, which left me free to look for work. Fortunately she settled in well. Now four and a half, she was a bright, friendly vivacious child who soon made friends.

Life in London seemed to have lost all meaning for me now. The highly motivated ambitious person I once was had vanished. What was left was a hollow shadow of a woman concerned only with survival, and keeping my head above water. A black pall of misery appeared to hang over me. Soon after moving into the flat on the top floor of an Edwardian house, my parents arrived for a visit. At the same time I developed mumps, which Melanie, as carrier, picked up at school. Meanwhile the lease on the Maida Vale flat had run out, and with the tenants gone I needed to clean it thoroughly, which somehow I managed to do with my face like a balloon. With my mother unused to domestic work, and incapacitated by a sprained ankle, sustained in the narrow lanes of Venice, I knew there would be no help from that quarter. I remained in a deeply depressed state, and one evening, after watching a Woody Allen film, I leant against the railings staring at the River Thames close to Putney Bridge, until a passer-by actually said to me "Don't do it!"

With work beginning to come in the form of TV commercials, television and radio, I found an agency who supplied foreign au pair girls who would take a child to and from school and babysit, in exchange for board and lodgings. I didn't feel open to theatre work as Melanie needed me to be with her at bedtime. Over a period of four years we were home in London to half a dozen young women from Switzerland, Germany and France, bringing with them their diverse eccentricities and problems!

I had been at the birth of the anti-apartheid movement in England a few years earlier, growing from a small group of people meeting in the house of a South African trade union leader, and now I joined the local Putney group. After the massacre at Sharpeville, Paul Eddington, the actor, now a friend, wrote a stirring article in a Sunday newspaper urging an embargo on South African goods, which I and others took up. This was to have historic results. Nearly thirty years later the South African government made the decision to release Nelson Mandela as a result of the damage caused to the economy by the growing sanctions that were subsequently being imposed by the British and American governments against that apartheid regime.

That first summer back in England I took Melanie for a sad little holiday in Sussex, on beaches at Lancing, Shoreham and Worthing, being painfully aware of the seemingly happy families surrounding us. I took a job teaching acting at the Aida Foster Theatre School, and later that year I appeared in an extravaganza, a tribute to the colonies, called *Cavalcade of Commonwealth*, at the

Mermaid Theatre, with actors from Commonwealth countries giving individual performances. Representing South Africa, I appeared as Shakespeare's Juliet waking from her drugged sleep to find Romeo dead beside her. The highlight of the evening was Dame Sybil Thorndike's speech from Shaw's *St Joan*, a part she had made famous in her youth. I longed to talk to her during rehearsals, as she had known Michael, but I was too much in awe to approach her. At the party that followed, I met the actor who would become a lover until he was elected a Labour MP, when I had to be abandoned for the sake of expediency! After the performance I was given a lift home by Richard Baker, the well-known broadcaster, who had compered the show.

At the start of the following year I began to teach drama at the Corona Stage School in Chiswick. I later joined the cast of a play, *S For Scandal*, by an American dramatist, John O'Hare, understudying the lead, Sonia Dresdell. John toured with us round the country, and he and I had time for romantic dinners, and talks long into the night. He was an extremely loquacious Irish American, with a partiality for bourbon whiskey taken from a constantly well-filled hipflask. Melanie was taken to Sunderland at this time by my parents, where my mother had family, and we met up when our production arrived at the Empire Theatre there. Meanwhile after the tour ended, John visited me each night during my next engagement in *Love From a Stranger* at the Richmond

Theatre, before we left for Cambridge. At the end of that tour I returned to London to see John off on his return to the States. Arriving at the terminal, I discovered to my shocked surprise he had a wife in tow!

That summer Melanie and I travelled on the *Britannia Express* to the Hook of Holland, then through Holland, Austria and Germany to Italy. We took a local train to Udine and then a coach to Grado on the Ligurian coast. Emelio from Milan took to showing me the local sights, the open-air nightclub, Roman excavations at Aquilia, Miramare Castle, then a visit to Trieste and a nostalgic return to Venice. It was pleasant to have an Italian boyfriend to take me out, to wine and dine me. I was beginning to feel human again. I was able to leave Melanie to play happily (I hoped) on the beach with a British couple and their children we had just met. It seemed that I was belatedly sowing my wild oats after having met and married at such a young age. I was lonely, I needed a male friend, but I wasn't going to get involved emotionally. I had been too deeply wounded by Michael's death. I had closed down and shut off my heart. I had barely participated in the sexual freedom of theatre life, but now there was a growing social sexual freedom to be explored.

I had become determined to master the Italian language, which I had always loved, ever since learning to sing in Italian, and taking lessons in Ipswich ten years earlier. I needed to have regular employment, and took the job of drama teacher two or three days a week at Dulwich College Prep School, where I produced a puppet performance of *A Christmas Carol*, which was good therapy for some of the shy, repressed little boys. At the same time I managed to do a TV commercial with Hughie Green, and then started rehearsals for a new play, *Lizard on the Rock*, with Harry Andrews, which opened at the Phoenix Theatre and closed after two weeks. Fortunately I went straight into rehearsals for a BBC television drama production called *Bonehead*, transmitted live from the Lime Grove Studios in Shepherd's Bush.

About this time I was becoming involved with Geoffrey, a blue-eyed golden-haired young man I had met in the Italian class. (He told me I had the best legs of any of the women there!) He had an Italian partner, he said, but wanted to get out of the relationship. I in turn enjoyed the attention of a good-looking young man. He began to turn up at my flat, uninvited, in his blue van at any time of day or night. He even turned up at the Alexandra Theatre in Birmingham where I was rehearsing for a performance of *Murder at the Vicarage*. We spent part of the afternoon in Stratford-on-Avon and the night in a hotel in Warwick. He left me at five a.m. to pay the bill so he could be back in London in time for work!

In September Melanie and I took a train for Italy again. At Ventimiglia we were met at the station by

Sylvia, a former au pair, now a friend, who took us by bus to Diano Marina on the southern coast where she was working as a tourist guide. On our way home we managed to see Monte Carlo and visited a casino, before travelling to Paris to stay with Sylvia's Moroccan boyfriend in a primitive old building with a communal toilet on the landing consisting only of a hole in the floor. After flushing one had to get to the door fast before the floor flooded.

Something of a melodrama occurred sometime later. Geoffrey had appeared one lunchtime when Melanie happened to be off school sick, so I invited him to join us for lunch. There was a knock on the door, and on opening it I found a young woman on the doorstep. "Are you Mrs Thompson?" and "Is Geoffrey here?" I had barely answered in the affirmative when all hell broke out. With a shriek she threw herself at me dragging her nails down my cheeks, drawing blood. I hastily retreated to the kitchen with this Italian virago hot on my heels. The next moment she was grabbing hold of the bread knife sitting on the bread board and brandishing it menacingly. I didn't stop to witness her next step, instead I grabbed hold of Melanie and raced for the door, down two flights of stairs, and out into the back garden to hide in the far bushes. On the way round the side of the house I had glimpsed a pushchair with a small child ensconced. We waited hidden in the garden for some time in a state of silent fear, only communicating in whispers. Finally, on venturing out I noticed the pushchair had gone. With a visibly scratched and bloody face I continued on to a nearby park with Melanie. I wasn't ready to go home just yet.

About that time I was recording for a Sid James show at the TV Centre followed by recording *Stories From World History* at the BBC World Service based at Portland Place. I also auditioned for the endless *Mousetrap* at the Ambassador Theatre. There was a time when I supplied some of the voices for Lotti Lenegar's shadow puppet play for television, together with two well-known members of the *Carry On* films team, who made me laugh a lot. I loved radio work, perhaps because I had been part of that medium in South Africa before ever meeting Michael, whereas performing in the theatre or on television meant little to me now with no one to appraise me. My career had become a way of making a living only. Actors have a need to prove themselves to an audience. This sense of insecurity often stems from a lack of love or encouragement as a child, as was my experience. However well I appeared to do I continued to lack confidence.

On New Year's Eve of that year, 1963, Geoffrey called round just as I was leaving, later than I intended, to get a train to a party in Richmond. He rather reluctantly offered to drive me there instead. Despite his partner's attempt to kill me we had continued with our affair. We had an Israeli girl, named Nira, staying with us at that time, and before she left she admitted that Geoffrey had been "paying her attention too" while I was away working. He had been calling on her that night, as I was to be out. He was probably servicing three women at the same time. That was the final straw for me!

The year 1964 proved a very busy one for me. In February I began rehearsals for a Tennessee Williams play *Period of Adjustment*. In the cast were Donald Sutherland, who was to return to Canada to make his name in films, and Nigel Hawthorne, a fellow-South African, who later made his name in *Yes Minister* and *The Madness of King George*. I played Donald's wife, with a southern American accent, and one scene opened with us in bed together, which I found quite difficult. I don't think I was uninhibited enough at that time to play such an intimate scene on stage! I had to take a day off rehearsals in the first week in order to record another episode from *Stories From World History* for the BBC. While playing at Bromley at night, I began to participate in a series of classes for actors at the Royal Court Theatre led by William Gaskell, exploring mask work, clowning and improvisation, among other experimental forms. George Devine, running the theatre at that time, and Laurence Olivier were additional teachers at some of the sessions. I still remember Sir Laurence urging us to practise looking out of the back of our heads! The mask work we practised involved selecting a half mask from a large collection of different masks, looking at one's face in a mirror, finding that character's clothes and any props it might use, then on developing its own distinctive walk and voice walking on stage to interact with other characters. This process might be repeated with another mask, while continuing to improvise. What I found was that each character seemed to have a life of its own, an exciting and terrifying experience at the same time. Keith Johnson, who went on to write about the work he witnessed, and Peter Gill, later a theatre director, were involved as writers on the side lines. I continued to attend classes whenever I could over a period of many months. It was a stimulating, informative and sometimes frightening experience. At the end of April we did a performance at the Royal Court Theatre for a live audience.

My next engagement was a season of repertory at Ilfracombe. I thought it would be good for Melanie and me to get out of London and live by the coast for the summer. It meant taking her away from her school for the last six weeks of the summer term, but I hoped it wouldn't affect her as a nine-year-old. I managed to enrol her in a school in Ilfracombe, and unfortunately her maths schooling never recovered. Although weekly rep, learning a new part each week, was particularly hard work, we managed to have fun, sharing a flat with Sheila, a friendly young stage manager. On Mel's birthday, my parents, who were meanwhile living in Bournemouth for a while, took her to Butlins in Minehead, a bus journey away. She hated it! A child had drowned in the pool the week before, so she wasn't allowed to swim. My parents didn't know how to enjoy themselves, resulting in a miserable ninth birthday. To make up for it, at the end of the summer season, we flew back to Italy to stay with friends Peter and Jill from my Ipswich theatre days, who had settled in Barga, a small hilltop town in Tuscany. We were accompanied by my sister-in-law Brenda and baby son Daniel. We explored the nearby town of Lucca, and Florence, and crossed the mountains to get to the sea at Marina di Massa. As always I felt good in Italy. Maybe Italy is my spiritual home.

Back in London, I began to look for a flat or house to buy. I was drawn to Bristol as the city had the first comprehensive schools, the form of education I wanted for my daughter. Moreover, Val May, with whom I had worked at Ipswich, and whose wife had had a room in my flat before they married, was running the Bristol Old Vic Theatre. Meeting the two of them for lunch on a cold January day, I learned that the company were on contracts till the end of the year, so there was no possibility of my joining just then. Nevertheless I went ahead with an interview with the head of drama at Bristol BBC, and viewed a couple of houses. (The houses were large three-storey period buildings priced at just over £2,000, in Clifton, now probably worth millions!)

In May we moved into a top-floor flat in a fine Victorian house in Putney, the forty-year lease of which was covered completely by the money paid out by the insurance company on Michael's death. The only money Michael left was £500 in a bank account. Due to his weak heart he was unable to take out a life insurance policy, but when he joined Television Wales and the West a few months before he died, he automatically joined their insurance scheme, with no health questions asked. I was to remain in that flat for twenty-one years. What meant so much to me about living in Putney were the open spaces. There was the mysterious hidden pond on Wimbledon Common, Putney and Barnes Common close to the Thames, and much-loved Richmond Park, where Joan and I would meet up with our children and her dogs for chaotic picnics on a Sunday. Close contact with nature had always been important to me, and I dreamed of one day living in the country.

Meanwhile I continued to play parts in dramas for BBC overseas and schools radio, playing Amy Johnson the aviator, and then repeating the part again on another occasion (broadcasts were always live, programmes weren't recorded at that time), and Eliza Doolittle from *Pygmalion*. There was some more work in TV and commercials, and a small part in John Schlesinger's film *Darling*, with Julie Christie. When the red warning bills came in, threatening to cut off gas or electricity in so many days, there would somehow always be a repeat commercial payment turning up from some obscure TV station, and the day would be saved! During this time I took weekly classes in mime with Claude Chagrin, one of Jacques Lecoq's teachers, Lecoq the French mime artist. Steven Berkoff was a fellow-student.

Diana Roberts, an old friend of Michael's and a passionate balletomane, would treat Melanie and me to a seat at the Royal Opera House, usually in the front stalls because of her bad eyesight. Diana lived in a building in Irving Street, Leicester Square, five double flights up. The lift had stopped working years ago and never been fixed. As a former director of a children's theatre, she became in mature years a surrogate mother to me, and a number of ballet dancers, including Wayne Sleep, who later became our friend. There was always a meal and a rest on offer when I was in town seeing agents, or doing a broadcast. Once a year I would take her out for a meal on her birthday, the day after Michael's birth-and-death day. After celebrating a special birthday party, I left the restaurant with Wayne Sleep to go on to a nightclub, where we had fun dancing together with abandon. She never married, having lost the love of her life, Warren Jenkins, to another woman. She was a great friend to me, and was influential in getting me a small weekly child benefit from Actors' Equity. She died long ago, but I miss her still. Another memorable time was the opportunity to see Peter Brook's famous productions of *Marat/Sade* and *A Midsummer Night's Dream* in an all-white set, at the Aldwych Theatre and participate in master classes for actors with him.

Soon after moving into the new flat in Ravenna Road I met Desmond, and one night he came round with a bottle of champagne to celebrate his landing a new job in commercial advertising. When I was unable to summon up any enthusiasm for his appointment, he lost his rag, and proceeded to pour the champagne over me, which was the end of that brief affair! I am reminded of the first time I was introduced to the stuff, when as a seventeen-year-old ingénue actress, on tour in South Africa, a young fan who had attached himself to our theatre company arrived at my bedroom door to wake me the first morning in my Durban hotel with a bottle of champagne. It felt terribly romantic!

A New Beginning, Another Ending

In June of 1964, Sheila, of the Ilfracombe Company, brought round Martin, a young friend of hers to babysit for us, and soon he was spending more and more time at the flat. Although there were fourteen years between us (he was only nineteen), we got on extremely well, and the relationship grew. My friends liked him, he was charming and fun to be with. He was also very good looking, and had been a male model at one time. Until I met Martin, I realised later, I had probably been clinically depressed for seven years. That's how Melanie remembers me. I now began to enjoy life again. The following year Martin and I decided to hitch round my beloved Italy, from Rome to Naples, then on to Ischia, Sorrento and Amalfi. We managed to get a lift to Salerno in the south from where we visited the Roman ruins at Paestum. Then back to Rome and Orvieto, a train to Florence, and a bus to Barga to visit Gill and Peter, old friends from Ipswich Theatre days. Later they were to set up Opera Barga, presenting seasonal productions of operas with recognised singers in a formerly abandoned theatre, which they renovated.

When Martin's parents moved from Harrow to Somerset, he moved into my flat, and that summer he took me to meet them. They were quite elderly with Lancashire accents, so different from Martin, whose temperament and looks were more Mediterranean. This was when I learned that he was an adopted child. In his job, at that time, as a car-hire chauffeur, he was befriended by Sandy Wilson, the writer and dramatist famous for his musicals *The Boy Friend* and *Valmouth*. We began to be invited to his flat off Gloucester Road for dinner and parties. There we met a number of famous personalities including Kenneth Tynan and his wife Kathleen.

On 30th March 1966 Martin and I were married. Like Michael, he was the one who pressed for marriage. He enjoyed our home life, it gave him the security he needed. I went along with it, but this time with some doubts. He was twenty-one and I was thirty-five. Neither of us looked our age, he looked older and I younger, but with a view to the future I had joked that there might come a time when he would be pushing me in a wheelchair! However I did care for him very much and maintained that he was the most mature man I had ever met, with a deep questioning intellect. He was generous, friendly, warm and confident. He had a way of drawing people to him of all ages, young and old. I was touched that he wanted to be with me. There had been an isolated incident shortly before the wedding when I considered calling it all off, but I was aware of the effect that would have on his parents, on Melanie and friends. There was also the fact that Sandy Wilson, our main witness, had gone to Brighton and was not contactable. Martin had shown a violent side I had not suspected, which had frightened me and caused Melanie to race up two flights of stairs from the garden in response to my scream. So I decided to go ahead with the wedding at Kensington Register Office with just Martin's parents, Melanie, Sandy Wilson and old friend Joan attending. I was glad to be part of a family again, while Melanie adored having Martin as a stepfather. We shared Martin's love of the Beatles and his record collection of jazz musicians, and he spent time with Melanie teaching her judo.

The next month we hired a small motor-powered cruiser at Chichester for a holiday. We decided to stick close to the coast at first and ventured up the estuary to Buckland Hard and Beaulieu. We knew there were picturesque stopping-off places, pleasant pubs and the famous motor museum. Martin had been quite confident about taking charge of the vessel, assuring me he knew all about boats. He seemed to know what he was doing, until he fell backward into the water while trying to start the engine. A few hours later, after dropping anchor in the harbour at Buckland Hard, and a pleasant extended lunch, we returned to find the tide had turned leaving the boat high and dry in a sea of mud. We were forced to wade out in bare feet through oozy mud and wriggling worms to get back on board for the night. We spent the next few days exploring the New Forest and the Beaulieu estate, before returning to the Solent. It was a lovely day, and the Isle of Wight looked so close that one could almost reach out and touch it. The sea was like a mill pond shimmering in the sunlight. With four days of our holiday left we decided to take the boat over to the island. Part way across the wind got up and choppy waves appeared. Suddenly there was a sickening lurch and a grinding sound, as though we had hit something. Rather belatedly we consulted the map. There were several shallows marked in the area. We were now being tossed around in mounting waves, while Melanie had crept to her bunk in terror. More by good luck than good judgement we managed to make the harbour at Cowes where we had difficulty in finding a mooring as the regatta was imminent. A few days later we returned to the harbour, and in spite of a strong wind blowing we set off to cross the Solent back to Chichester, as the boat was due back that day. The first thing I did was to make a pot of tea while Martin started her up. Before we were even out of the harbour the boat was lurching violently. I clung to the teapot as the contents of the mugs spilled over the table and floor. "Turn the bloody boat round and go back," I yelled, with the pain of the scalding water. I'd had enough! The next day Melanie and I took a ferry to

Southampton, then a train to London, while Martin waited for the owner to fetch his boat. He arrived back home later that night having had to compensate for a damaged keel.

In addition to classes in mime and Italian conversation I was now taking twice weekly dance classes, and by the end of the year I had started classes in comedy with Keith Johnson. On New Year's Day I began rehearsals for a BBC production of *The House on Canal Street*, and by April I began a full-time drama teaching job at the Arts Educational School, housed in a fine old building at Hyde Park Corner, where Beryl Grey, the ex-Royal Ballet dancer, was principal. The school was largely a training for dancers, but there was a drama department with two other teachers, where I taught the dance students voice production, mime and improvisation. When the weather was fine I would take them across into a secluded part of Green Park to work.

The Accident

In the summer holidays Melanie and I flew to Israel immediately after the '67 war, which then I seemed to have little awareness of what it had been about, and nobody we met seemed to talk about it. We joined my brother and sister-in-law camping on the shore of Galilee. Every afternoon the wind got up and by nightfall there was the sound of waves landing on the shore. I was reminded of the story of Jesus and his disciples in a boat on the lake when a storm blew up. Before I left home I had discovered I was pregnant, still within the first trimester. One day after returning to my brother's home in Haifa, we arranged to go on a picnic to the beach. I carried a heavy picnic basket, and began to haemorrhage. The bleeding continued through the night and the next morning we realised I was miscarrying.

There was a plan to visit the ruins at Caesarea that day, and rather than cancel the visit the family went ahead and left me to get on with it! After only one day to recover, I continued with Melanie on a planned itinerary to visit some friends who had settled in a kibbutz. From there we went on to Jerusalem where, like mad dogs and

Englishmen, we circumnavigated the walls of the Old City in the heat of the midday sun! We both loved the Old City with its mixture of nationalities, of Arab, Jewish, Christian and Armenian traditions, and somehow I seemed to survive the sightseeing itinerary.

On arriving back at Heathrow, expecting Martin to meet us, we received a message to say he had been delayed. After an anxious two-hour wait, he arrived. He had motored up from Somerset where he had been visiting his parents, and on the way the fan belt had broken. This was the sports car he had always dreamed of driving. He had traded in our Fiat 500 for a bright green Morgan convertible. He had done this while we were away, with help from his parents. Although I hadn't been consulted, he was obviously so thrilled to have it that I was happy for him.

In September I accompanied Martin to Stratford-on-Avon for an interview with the Royal Shakespeare Company as an assistant stage manager. A few days later he left to join their Theatre-Go-Round Company. Of course I was glad for him, but it came as a shock that he was leaving home to work. Through me and Sandy Wilson he had become interested in directing plays, and while I was away he had become involved with an alternative theatre company of young people taking a production to the Edinburgh Festival. He had been at Stratford for two weeks when I had a phone call from him saying he would be home at the weekend, that he had a cold through sleeping on someone's bare floor, and that he loved me. At 3.30 the next morning I was woken by a policeman shining a torch through my bedroom window. Martin had been seriously injured in a car accident! My immediate thought was that Melanie must not be disturbed. The policeman stood by me as I rang the hospital in Warwick where he had been taken. They confirmed that he had multiple head injuries and I should come as soon as possible. I lay on top of my bed in numb horror waiting for the dawn, when I could ring Joan to ask for help in getting to Warwick, and for child care. In spite of her car's broken exhaust pipe, which meant my sitting with my head out the window, we made it that morning to the hospital.

On arrival at the hospital we were met by a doctor who confirmed that Martin had sustained multiple head injuries and a broken wrist from a car accident. There was no hope of recovery. In this nightmare scenario I realised I would now have to inform his parents. How do you tell fond parents that their son is expected to die? It was the most difficult task I had ever been called upon to do. I spent the next few hours standing in a dingy corridor near the entrance door waiting for them to arrive. It was an agonising time. No one approached me, no one spoke to me during the hours of waiting. As soon as his parents arrived they asked to see Martin, something I hadn't even considered doing. I didn't join them. We were offered a room with three camp beds for the night, awaiting the final call to his bedside. We barely spoke, each numbed by our isolated misery. The next morning it was decided that as he was on a life-sustaining machine and therefore might survive for another few days, we should collect his belongings from where he had been staying and leave the hospital. It was now time for me to say goodbye. I would have to get back home to Melanie. I stood at the foot of Martin's bed barely recognising the figure that lay there with his bandaged head and sustaining tubes. My impression was that he was not there, that he had already gone. I whispered goodbye, and left.

We drove to Martin's accommodation to gather up his belongings, and discovered it to be an annex of an Elizabethan mansion belonging to Peter Hall, the theatre director, and Leslie Carron, his wife at that time. From there I continued on to Somerset with Martin's parents, staying overnight before getting a train back to London. Five days later Martin was certified dead. His mother had requested he be taken off the life machine as that was all that was keeping him alive. The following day my old friend John Wiles, who by this time was now living round the corner from me, drove me to Stratford-on-Avon, first to the police station to receive a statement, then on to the coroner's court for an official inquiry.

After the coroner's hearing, we decided to drive to Coventry to visit Warren Jenkins, the current director at the theatre there, who had directed me at Ipswich and become a friend. We found ourselves having dinner with him and wife Jenny and stayed on to see a production of *Caesar and Cleopatra*, before returning to London in the early hours of the morning. Three days later it was back to the same area for the funeral at a crematorium near Coventry. In addition to some of Martin's young friends and my older ones, there was a small group from the Stratford Theatre-Go-Round Company including the theatre director, Trevor Nunn. His parents collected the ashes, and I returned to London for the wake at my Putney flat, a party with close friends and music that Martin loved. An incongruous incident occurred when a couple of young gate crashers appeared at the door, and had to be informed that this was no ordinary party but a celebration of the life of an extraordinary young man.

I arranged a meeting with the stage manager, who had survived the crash. From him I learned what had happened. After Martin had rung me that night, it was decided over a drink with him and his American fiancée that they would drive out to visit a friend of theirs who needed cheering up after a broken relationship. They bought a bottle of wine to take with them and invited the young barmaid at the pub to accompany them. Apparently there was no reply when they knocked at the door of the spurned lover on arriving there, so they left. It appears he was in the bathroom at the time and failed to hear them. It was on the return journey, at a notoriously dangerous S bend, that the accident occurred. The sports car mounted a bank, turned over and then bounced back onto its wheels, throwing out its occupants, with its headlights still blazing. The stage manager was thrown free on to the road, with only slight injuries, the barmaid was knocked unconscious, the fiancée was killed outright, crushed by the car which landed on her, and Martin was thrown into a hedge by the force of a blow to the back of the head by the bar of the open hood. I was reminded them of Martin's prophetic words that he knew he would die one day at the wheel of a car. He couldn't have guessed it would be so soon!

It wasn't till after his death that I was presented with Martin's shadow side. I learned that instead of earning his living as a night postal worker as I was led to believe, he was spending his time at a flat in Hampstead with young friends I didn't know. Six weeks later I arranged to see them, stopping on the way to buy a bottle of whiskey as an offering and support. It was a difficult meeting as it appeared that he had been having an affair with a young woman living there, who was unaware of my existence. On my return to the pub before getting a tube train home, I met a young Australian who invited me back to his flat. In my shattered emotional state I accepted, and spent the night sobbing in his bed. There had also been several incidents around money. After collecting his belongings at Stratford, his parents and I discovered my stained building society book, with several recent withdrawals while in his possession. I learned from my bank when questioning some cheques that Martin had asked about a loan, offering as security the lease of my flat. Fortunately he was refused. John Wiles admitted to lending him several hundred pounds. The week he was in Stratford the police had called at my flat with a court order for unpaid car fines. It was evident that as he was not earning, he was in need of day-to-day money. Needless to say my unhappiness was increased by these revelations. I began to feel that I had lost him well before his death. With my working during the day and his absence on nights during the week, we had seen little of each other in the last few months.

Keeping Busy

During this time I tried to keep going at my job with the Arts Educational School until one day I broke down in the staffroom, to the embarrassment of the other teachers, and was sent home for the day. I had told no one there of my bereavement. This was a particularly difficult time for Melanie to be losing a father for the second time in her childhood, just as she was starting secondary school. It had been a happy few years with Martin, whom she loved, and he her. On my revealing to her that he had died she had cried out "Come back, come back," which tore at my heart. The parents of the dead American fiancée attended the inquest at Stratford in November, and my heart was heavy at their loss. I felt such a responsibility for Martin's actions.

How was it possible that I should find myself a widow once again? Somehow I had to get on with my life. I was determined not to fall into the dark space in which I had spent the seven years before I met Martin. I started to go to the theatre again, and saw the memorable all-male version of *As You Like It*, with Ronald Pickup as Rosalind, and the definitive production of Anton

Chekov's *The Three Sisters*, with, if my memory serves me right, Margaret Leighton, Celia Johnson and Renée Asherson. Sandy, who remained a good friend, took me to see a production of his musical *The Boy Friend* at Guildford, then at Windsor, while accompanying him together with Ken Tynan and his wife Kathleen, to see the same musical at the Comedy Theatre. At Christmas we invited Wayne Sleep, the Royal Ballet dancer, to spend the day with us. Through good friend Diana, who had taken Wayne under her wing while still at the Royal Ballet School, he had made a friend of Martin and was affected by his death coming soon after that of a close dancer friend, Graham, in Australia.

Early the next year I was fortunate to see two memorable performances – Judi Dench in *Cabaret* at the Palace Theatre and Jean Forbes-Robertson in *Hedda Gabler*. In the summer holidays from my work at the Arts Ed, I took Melanie on a Club Mediterranean holiday in Italy. After a night in Paris, we had an overnight train journey to Donoratico on the coast. The holiday was a disaster as Melanie became quite ill soon after we arrived at our primitive thatched cottage in the woods. A doctor was sent for and ordered daily injections in her bottom. She was unable to eat any of the food that Club Mediterranean is famous for, and I didn't want to leave her for the many facilities it provided. Fortunately after ten days she was able to join a group of young people on a visit to Rome, where at an early age she experienced the

Italian male's obsession with bottom pinching! On leaving, we took a train to France and were met at Chambéry by Sylvia, our former au pair, who lived in Geneva, arriving at three in the morning. Sylvia was married to a Czech, and on our fourth day there the news broke that Russia had invaded Czechoslovakia. Of course her husband Danyk was deeply affected by the news.

During that year of 1968 I joined in demonstrations against the Vietnam War and clashed with police outside the American Embassy in Grosvenor Square. In September I began work with Associated Television, and in December appeared in a Weekend Television production of *The Inner Man*, and four days of filming the following year at Shepperton Studios for *The Severed Head*, directed by Richard Attenborough and starring Ian Holm and Lee Remick. This was the year that I became involved with Group 64, a flourishing youth theatre based in a converted church conveniently at the bottom of my road. I began by offering weekly voice and mime classes, followed by rehearsals for a production of *The Promise*, with a cast of three. I had seen the play at the Fortune Theatre with the three characters played by Ian McKellen, Judi Dench and Ian McShane, and was deeply impressed by it. The story of three young people's fight for survival at the time of the Siege of Leningrad, moved me on a deep level. I used parts of Shostakovich's Eleventh Symphony, written and performed there at that time, to highlight the situation and add atmosphere to the

Russian background. The weather was particularly cold on the night of the first performance, so that the audience was given a taste of the desperate conditions in which the play was set.

With the establishment of the hippie era, I resorted to wearing long loose dresses bedecked with beads and bells, and walking barefoot down Putney High Street's dirty pavements! As a non-conformist I was making a statement that felt enormously freeing. As a teenager in Johannesburg I had been part of a bohemian group of pseudo-artists. Meanwhile Melanie and I were excited by the chance to see a production of *Hair*, the American rock musical, and eagerly joined the cast on stage when invited to dance together with them at the finale! Opening at the end of theatre censorship, the production brought a refreshing openness with its criticism of the Vietnam War, its stirring music and nudity. Needless to say it created a lot of controversy. A new phenomena of this period of Swinging London was Biba, the boutique that ostensibly provided the first fashion for teenagers. I enjoyed accompanying Melanie, now a teenager, to the shop in Kensington Church Street and later in Kensington High Street. The former presented a dark, mysterious boudoir interior, providing uniquely different clothes, and the first miniskirts and brightly coloured feather boas. We also made visits to Carnaby Street in Soho with boutiques promoting mod and hippie styles for Swinging London. Both these areas became prime tourist attractions in the next few years.

Meanwhile I continued to be offered parts in radio, television and in two feature films. In *Leo the Last*, directed by John Boorman, there was a memorable scene with Marcello Mastroianni in a swimming pool with about twenty others, all in the nude apart for flesh-coloured briefs. The scene was meant to represent one of the New Age therapies prevalent in California at that time. Placed behind Marcello, where I could see the face-lift scars behind his ears, we exchanged some words in his native Italian, when he was suddenly called by the director, and kicking off strongly to swim across the pool, his foot landed right in my fanny!

In May I began to assist John Wiles on his production of Sartre's *The Flies* at Group 64, and the following year on his dramatisation of the voyages of Ulysses. John had been the stage manager of the touring company in which I had played ingénue parts in South Africa after leaving school. As I was the baby of the company he had taken me under his wing, and looked after me. He arrived in England soon after I did, and made a name for himself as a writer of novels, plays and TV scripts, including regularly writing for *Z Cars*. His book *Leap for Life*, relating his work through movement and theatre productions with delinquent boys, broke new ground. He assembled large numbers of children in his productions, and his enthusiasm for his work became an inspiration to drama and dance teachers in Britain. Using his well-tried methods on Group 64's young actors (Melanie having become one of them), his productions were a great success. In the summer, Melanie and I joined John at the Edinburgh Festival, watching several productions each day, with a memorable performance of Ibsen's *The Wild Duck*, with Mai Zetterling. I could only ever refer to the play thereafter with a Swedish accent!

At the end of that year Melanie and I were deeply impressed by Dennis Potter's play *The Son of Man* at the Roundhouse in Camden Town. At the performance conclusion, with the actor playing Jesus left nailed to the cross, we continued to sit, transfixed in our seats, till we were gently ushered out, being reassured that the character would rise from the dead in three days' time!

Melanie at Diano Marina, aged seven, 1962

PART THREE
1970–1979

The Meditation Student and Yoga Teacher

Spiritual Awakening

Teaching

I had been advised by John Allen, drama adviser for the British Council, to train as a drama teacher at a teachers' training college in order to be officially recognised, so I took his advice and started a two-year course at Whitelands, a college conveniently within walking distance from my flat in Putney. When I subsequently found that my practical knowledge of drama exceeded that of the lecturers, I opted for the English course instead. A highlight of the first year was an arranged visit to Summerhill, the famous progressive school set up by the legendary AS Neill. I have a mental picture today of a collection of naked young bodies flinging themselves into a pool in the grounds, as I travelled up the drive. I was delighted to be able to meet and question Neill on his ideas for education, and found him a warm, caring man. Meanwhile I directed a production of *Under Milk Wood* with my adult education students, and *Hobson's Choice* later that year. In the summer holidays I chose to study James Joyce for my course and arranged to visit Dublin to participate in a week of lectures on the writer, which entailed viewing all the sites that Bloom visited over a period of one day in *Ulysses*. At the end of an enjoyable course, I met up with an old theatre friend working on a TV assignment in Dublin, and stayed with him for a few days at his cottage in Dalkey, high up overlooking the sea. We enjoyed a visit to the Abbey Theatre for a production of Brendan Behan's play *The Hostage*, and at the weekend a wonderful drive to Silver Sands in County Wicklow. This was my first experience of Irish lakes and mountains, and I was completely captivated.

Later that summer of 1971 I had my first camping experience with some young people from Group 64, the youth theatre, in the New Forest near Ringwood. I loved it! One day I took my clothes off and lay in the bracken sunbathing, when to my horror I noticed a snake slithering by, while on another occasion I saw a man on a white horse galloping towards me where I lay equally exposed among the tall grass, and was forced to sit up to reveal myself in order to prevent a serious accident. Fortunately I didn't seem to frighten the horse too much!

By the end of the holidays I had made a decision not to go back to college. My experience in a London comprehensive school had put me off the idea of teaching drama in schools, forever. Instead I got on with directing a production of *Look Back in Anger* at Group 64 early the following year. The next month I went into rehearsals for Anouilh's *Ring Round the Moon*, a play I loved, having played the Clare Bloom part at the theatre in Ipswich. I was really enjoying the position of director, with the power it gave to be creative within a larger picture, instead of in the actor's role of interpreter. On Saturdays I was teaching drama improvisation classes at Group 64, and during the week classes for teachers, while attending yoga and philosophy classes for myself. I had worked with my body most of my life, so took to yoga asanas like a duck to water.

During this year of 1971, David, a young lost poet, suffering from a recently broken relationship, and seventeen years my junior, became a friend and then lover after moving in with me. We were two unhappy souls in need of some stability. About this time a life insurance policy matured, the premiums of which I had continued to pay after Michael's death. I had always wanted to live in the country and now decided to buy a country cottage with the money, all £2,000 of it! Gloucestershire seemed a suitable area for a cheap cottage. I began by visiting estate agents in Stroud. I spent all of July staying in a friend's idyllic cottage in the Cotswolds, where Melanie and her friends were able to visit, before doing a tour that took David and me across the border to theatre friends in Wales, where we bought a tent in Monmouth and camped in the Wye Valley, while on my search for a cottage. Set in a Forest of Dean village, I found the perfect place – a simple whitewashed period cottage with magnificent views across a valley to the distant Black Mountains. I made an offer without ever seeing inside it! What I was able to see of the only downstairs room, through its three windows, was sufficient. I loved what I saw. Although I still had to find another £1,000 to pay for it (I had no knowledge of mortgages and as a woman probably couldn't have applied for one anyway), my offer was accepted. In October, with the help of friends, I moved furniture down to Lydbrook. The 120-mile journey along the A40 from southwest London seemed like no problem at all. I had recently learned to drive and was in the possession of a little green car called Beth, short for Bethnal Green. I was at last fulfilling a dream I had of being the owner of a country cottage. This one needed a lot of work before I could contemplate living in it, but I intended spending every weekend I could in preparation for that day.

That September, on the advice of my yoga teacher, Penny Neal-Smith, I began a yoga teacher training course. Yoga had been a life-saver for me. Its practice gave me a sense of calm and peace that I had rarely if ever experienced before. The emotional wounds created by the deaths of both husbands were beginning to be healed. I wanted the opportunity of passing on such benefits to the drama students I was teaching. Not only was the practice increasing my physical stamina, but I could feel the effect on a mental, emotional and spiritual level. In May the following year I started to teach my first yoga class. The yoga master BKS Iyengar arrived in England from India to give lectures and demonstrations as well as classes for yoga teachers. Iyengar was greatly revered and respected, and yet somehow managed to strike fear in the hearts of his students. When I asked his permission to become a serious yoga teacher, he seemed to look into my very soul before answering. Yes, I might start initially with a couple of classes a week. I continued to train with him on his visits to London over the next few years. On one occasion, while standing on my head, I suddenly became aware of a feeling of nausea brought on by having eaten some refrozen melted ice-cream before the class, and was forced to make a dash for the toilets. His voice followed me bellowing "No one leaves my class, whatever the circumstance!" I was in disgrace! Yet within a few weeks I was teaching four, then six, then eight, and finally twelve yoga classes a week for the Inner London Education Authority, and thoroughly enjoying it. With the acceptance of a new alternative lifestyle, out went lipstick, high heels, coffee, white sliced bread and sugar, and in came wholemeal bread, brown rice, dandelion coffee, cotton clothing, honey and pure cosmetics.

At Covent Garden, Melanie and I were taken to see Margot Fonteyn and Rudolf Nureyev in their historic performance of *Romeo and Juliet*. Sitting in the stalls, we were so close to the stage that I experienced Nureyev's sweat fly off him as he performed a succession of pirouettes downstage. This was an exciting period of ballet performances with the inspired couple dancing together in *Giselle*, *Swan Lake*, *Les Sylphides* and

Marguerite and Armand. There were also wonderful performances from premier dancers Christopher Gable, Lynn Seymour, Antoinette Sibley and Merle Park.

In May 1972 I was approached by Jack Alcock to take on his adaptation of *The Good Soldier Schweik*. He was keen to play the title role. I was familiar with the original story and was interested in directing it. The idea was initially to perform the play *The Good Soldier Schweik Goes to War* at Group 64 and then go on tour. I meanwhile auditioned actors and began rehearsals while Jack arranged the tour. Unfortunately he managed to come up with only one booking, in Littlehampton, and also proved to be a poor actor. When he made a derogatory remark to an actor during rehearsals concerning his homosexuality, I walked out in disgust. After that I refused to work with him, and less than two weeks before opening found myself looking for a replacement. Fortunately I discovered that in the perfect casting of Michael Balfour, who with a lot of persuasion agreed to take on the part. There was certainly nothing in it for him except the chance to play a wonderful character part. With the production heavily reliant on cut-out props and scenery I had the added problem of an incompetent stage manager. I had had to take whoever I could as there was no money available for the rehearsal period. Needless to say there were no further bookings, and I felt sorry for the actors who had worked so very hard for such little return. My fingers were burned and I had learned a salutary lesson!

By the beginning of the following year I had started to attend two pottery classes a week at Putney Art School, while I was teaching a weekly drama class at a theatre school, and rehearsing Dennis Potter's *Son of Man* at the Youth Theatre. I managed to get down to the cottage in Lydbrook most weekends and in the summer, after working for two weeks with technical staff making a film for television, I was able to spend the whole of August working on the cottage with partner David, and having time to get to know the very beautiful Wye Valley and Forest of Dean.

Melanie at this time had become a student of dance and theatre at Dartington College of Arts in south Devon. She had auditioned at the London Central School of Drama and the Old Vic School in Bristol, but had opted for the more experimental teaching methods and work at Dartington. Interestingly her father had talked of a desire to send her to the original school there. He had visited Dartington Hall when involved with the Kurt Jooss Ballet Company, who had had a placement at Dartington, through his position of manager of Joan Littlewood's legendary Theatre Workshop in Manchester in the 1940s. Melanie had started performing at Group 64, the youth centre housed in a converted church at the bottom of our road, when she was fourteen, and attending workshops at the Oval House, a community youth project run by Peter Oliver, a dedicated man. It was at the Oval House that early experimental theatre began to flower with the help of such people as Nola Rae, Nancy Meckler, and Siobhan Davies, with clowning, theatre and dance, while groups such as Shared Experience, Pip Simmons, and the People Show, began life there. It was an exciting time in physical theatre, and a whole new integrated arts practice.

Namgyal Rinpoche

In March 1974 I had a meeting with a meditation teacher that was to have a profound influence on the rest of my life. I had been given a lift by a friend to Saffron Walden to hear Namgyal Rinpoche give a talk at Kham Tibetan House, a Tibetan Buddhist centre. As we had arrived at the end of his talk he kindly invited us to follow him back to his hotel room in Newmarket. A couple of years earlier I had been fortunate to hear him give a talk at my old friend Marie's flat in Hampstead. At that time I took with me Melanie and a couple of friends. I had felt an affinity with him that evening. He was talking my language, expressing what I had long believed but hadn't the words for. Here was the meditation teacher I had been seeking, ever since becoming involved in yoga. My study of yoga had already set me on a spiritual path and this was the next step. It is said that when the student is ready the teacher appears. Soon after, this six-foot-seven Canadian returned to Canada to his dharma centre in Ontario. Many years earlier, in 1956, after attending a talk in London given by the Venerable U Thilda Sayadaw, a Burmese meditation teacher, Lesley George Dawson, as

he then was, travelled to Burma to study with this
teacher. "Keep the routine of your life simple," he was
told, "and focus on the quest of direct insight above all
else. Rules and rituals are not of any importance.
Enlightenment alone is the aim of Buddhist life." He went
on to receive ordination and became known as Bhikkhu
Ananda Bodhi. The bhikkhu spent five years studying in
Burma, Thailand and Sri Lanka, and was eventually
recognised as a master teacher of the dharma. In 1961 the
English Sangha Association asked him to become the
incumbent abbot in London. During the next few years
he gave extensive teaching throughout the UK and
established the Hampstead Buddhist Vihara in London,
and a retreat centre in the south of Scotland called
Johnstone House. When Akong Rinpoche, Chime
Rinpoche and Chögyam Trungpa Rinpoche arrived in
Britain as Tibetan refugees, he was responsible for
assisting Trungpa in founding the first Tibetan Buddhist
meditation monastery in the West, by handing over the
property of Johnstone House, used at that time by his
students. It was to become Samye Ling, a thriving karma
Kagyu centre. He returned to Canada in 1965 where he
began teaching in Toronto, and the following year set up
the Dharma Centre of Canada in a 400-acre property
near Kinmount in Ontario as a meditation centre. For
eight months of the year he continued to teach in
Canada, and for the remaining four months encouraged
students to travel and study with him. During one of

these many trips, on visiting His Holiness the Sixteenth Karmapa at Rumtek in Sikkhim, he was recognised as the reincarnation of the famous saint, Nyingma Lama Ju Mipham Namgyal Rinpoche, and was officially enthroned. Many of his students were young Canadians of the hippie era, a time of experimenting with drugs and challenging traditions. He realised they required something other than traditional Buddhist meditation, so he began to use a wide range of approaches to awakening using psychotherapy, Western science, art, philosophy, psychology, movement and dance together with other disciplines. In this rich experimental time he investigated what activities would most help liberate beings. Now he was back in this country, and I was sitting on his bed while he occupied the only chair, and we were conversing like friends! Unaware of his status I wasn't yet in awe of this charismatic teacher. That would come later. "If you want to practise meditation come to Canada in the summer for a six-week meditation course I shall be giving at the Dharma Centre." As a lonely, unhappy child I had had a strong inner life, and in conversing with God I had felt comforted and not so lonely. My father was a Christian Scientist, and I attended a Christian Science Sunday school from the age of eight. Through him I inherited a respect for and faith in the power of spiritual healing. Before I was born my father had had a profound healing, and had become a devoted student of Mary Baker Eddy, daily studying her *Science of Health With*

Key to the Scriptures together with the Bible. On the wall of our Christian Science church in Johannesburg were the words "You shall know the truth and the truth shall make you free". Together with Polonius's advice to his son Laertes – "This above all: to thine own self be true, / And it must follow, as the night the day, / Thou canst not then be false to any man" – I have always searched for the truth, when studying Stanislavsky as an actress, with his emphasis of finding the truth of a situation, as a yoga scholar, as a peace activist and later as a psychotherapist. Although Michael had been an atheist I had continued to believe in a spiritual component of life. Finding Namgyal Rinpoche felt like coming home, or like a big sigh of recognition! Now I was totally ready for self-exploration through meditation.

Canada

On returning to London I immediately booked a flight for myself and Melanie to Toronto for a six-week stay in August and September. Two weeks before leaving, a group of Rinpoche's students began arriving at my flat from Peru, where he had been teaching. Apparently my address had somehow been handed on to them as somewhere to stay in London! These were the senior students who were later to become leading international teachers themselves. "Why are you going to Canada, when the teacher is coming to Britain?" I was asked. The teacher had instructed me to go to Canada for a meditation course he said he was giving, and I didn't intend to change my plans. So we flew to Toronto to stay with Marie, who had meanwhile settled there, and to await news of Rinpoche's course at the Dharma Centre. The news came in the form of a phone call from London informing us of a ten-day meditation course taking place there in Ros Langdon's flat! Here I was thousands of miles from home awaiting my first meditation course and it was taking place in my own flat! All I could do was laugh, which is what I did, at the ridiculous situation.

Was this part of the teaching I needed – a loosening-up process before learning to meditate? How should we spend our time now? My brother Theo and his wife, living in Chicago at the time, were planning a visit to New York. Why didn't we join them? I had never been interested before in visiting the USA (I had been against America's political involvement in Korea and then Vietnam), but maybe I should now. When the train arrived at Grand Central Station we were met with placards announcing the resignation of the president, Richard Nixon! New York at that time was viewed as particularly dangerous, and we spent our time there in terror of being shot on the streets. After three days of sightseeing we were both relieved to leave on a train for Vermont, where we had been invited to stay with a friend among the forests and lakes. What a contrast! I managed while there to visit Tale of the Tiger, a meditation centre set up for Chögyam Trungpa Rinpoche, who had been one of the Tibetans who had taken over Johnson House in Scotland, later called Samye Ling, which had belonged to Namgyal Rinpoche's students in the 1960s. From Vermont we travelled on to Halifax in Nova Scotia to stay with Marcia, an American, who had lodged with us while studying at the Central School of Art some years before.

On arriving back in Toronto, this time staying with Cecilie, whom I had last seen working on course notes on my kitchen table at home, I decided to go up to the Dharma Centre in northern Ontario to await the arrival of the teacher. A friend of Melanie's had made it to Toronto and they planned to travel around doing street clowning, in which they had both trained. The centre consisted of a main house, a temple and a number of meditation huts in several hundred acres of land stretching to a lake, which I never managed to get to. I was expected to work while I was there, and I mucked in collecting wood from the forest and repainting the exterior of the temple in traditional Tibetan colours. I learned the joys of living with mosquitoes in midsummer and not being able to venture out without a covering of chemical spray. My hut was quite away from the main buildings, and one night I was woken by the sound of heavy scratching on the wooden door. With my heart thumping I got up and put a chair against it (there was no lock). The scratching continued, and as there were bears on the estate my fear was that one of them was trying to get in! I didn't dare go out that night to have my customary pee. Sure enough next morning I found deep scratch marks on the door. On relating the story of my night prowler it was suggested that it was probably a porcupine rubbing his quills on the wood. At the end of a week's stay I got a lift back to Toronto only to be met by Cecilie with the words "You might as well turn right around and go back to the centre. Rinpoche is expected to arrive in the morning." He had just docked at Montreal from Europe. In those days and for many subsequent years the teacher travelled from one continent to another by Polish cargo boat. He would take a number of students, usually eleven, with him, as twelve was the number of passengers accepted on any cargo boat, teaching daily classes on the journey – the world as classroom! He would arrive in a country, be it Britain, Switzerland, Germany, Japan, Australia or New Zealand, where he already had established centres, and the travelling students would augment those of the host group. The Namgyal had always been the traveller through many incarnations.

We spent that evening organising three buses to take most of his students up to the centre in the morning. What a wonderful welcoming party that was! After a short ceremony we enjoyed a celebratory feast, and while walking down the steps of the temple I met the teacher and expressed my pleasure that he was able to use my flat for his teachings. I expected him to thank me and say how sorry he was that I missed them, but all I got was a nod and the question of how much longer I was staying. I replied that I was booked on a plane in a couple of days' time. "Well then we'd better arrange a blessing for you in Toronto tomorrow so you can go ahead and practise." The following day about sixty people crammed into a small room (and I thought this was a blessing for me) on a particularly hot day. The Rinpoche conducted an empowerment of Chenrezig, the deity of compassion. The Dalai Lama is the embodiment of this deity. This, my first experience of a Tibetan ceremony, felt strangely familiar and comforting. It was to be the first of many in future years.

Namgyal Rinpoche

Mexico

The following day we flew home to London to find the flat still full of Canadians! The talk was of the therapy retreat the Rinpoche would be giving in Mexico in six weeks' time. Before I realised what I was doing I agreed to go too in spite of having no money left. Somehow, in the interim period, I was able to earn enough to pay the fare back to Canada, where I would travel down to Mexico with some of the dharma students. There would be practically no money available to pay for the course and dana donation (a voluntary payment in the Buddhist tradition) to the teacher, but I was persuaded that if the project was right the money would appear! Sure enough when the time came to leave, to my surprise, there was enough money in my account for the trip. And what a trip it turned out to be! After waiting around several days in Toronto for an old school bus to be repaired, we finally left on the most uncomfortable journey imaginable! The wooden seats were narrow and hard, and because we were late leaving we had to drive through the nights – five of them, sitting upright trying to sleep. We travelled down through the United States, with only food and pee stops. Even then we finally arrived at Malaque on the west coast of Mexico two days late. The journey wasn't uneventful. There were young children aboard who naturally became fretful, and tempers rose, until one member totally freaked out and had to be dumped! Although I found the journey exhausting, I loved the changing scenery and especially the dawn and evening sunsets. I remember the pleasure I had reading John Fowles' *The Magus* during those long days.

The site was beautiful – a hotel on the beach with more than a hundred Canadians, Americans, and a handful or two of Europeans staying in another hotel or in huts nearby. What followed was the most unusual experience of my life! Every day we practised the de-armouring exercises devised by Alexander Lowen, took part in primal therapy, Gestalt exercises, and Reichian massage and breath work. At the start of each morning and in the evening we met for meditation with the teacher in an open-sided canopied area. There we also took part or acted as spectators in individual psychodramas set up with good and bad parent in each corner of what looked like a boxing ring. The protagonist would enact aspects of their life, while others would stand in for significant members of their life story. I think we were all moved by the real life dramas we witnessed.

During a Gestalt exercise on the beach one morning I was encouraged to express my feelings towards a young Canadian woman whom I knew had had an affair with

David in London while I was in Canada. We ended up wrestling in the sand, yelling and pulling each other's hair. Suddenly a Mexican policeman appeared on the scene preparing to arrest us. I was terrified, with visions of being flung into a Mexican jail to remain there indefinitely! Fortunately, Len, our Gestalt therapist doctor, managed to persuade him that we were only playing, with no intent to harm each other. To our relief he left after giving us a firm admonishment, and the two of us ended up becoming friends. On one occasion the teacher had us form a double line facing each other in the sea with arms forming an arch, while one by one we were expected to pass through the human tunnel remaining under water as long as we could. This turned out to be a representation of the birth/death experience. A more profound experience occurred after I had been lying in the foetal position on a mattress in one of the rooms we used for therapy, when, after several days of practising the bioenergetics exercises, which had the effect of opening one up energetically and emotionally, I began to cry desperately like a small baby. I lay on my back with fists on either side of my head and knees drawn up as a three-months-old baby. Through my closed lids I was aware of a small figure standing over my cot or pram holding something large and white. As it descended towards my face I managed to turn my head away with a great sense of fear. Then I heard the sound of a scream as if coming towards me through a tunnel – the primal scream. My mother used to recount with some pride the words of my brother Theo, two and a half years older than me: "She was crying, so I gave her something to cry for." He must have tried to shut me up by placing a pillow over my face, nearly killing me in the process. Meanwhile I had grown up with a Desdemona complex, with a fear of being smothered in bed. I even told my husband when we first married that I was afraid that he might smother me. Having relived the original trauma the fear left me forever. I actually wrote to my brother telling him of my experience, but mysteriously the letter never arrived!

We were given two free Sundays during that intense period. I spent some of the time snorkelling, and exploring the surrounding area, richly tropical in vegetation. Following a pathway to an adjoining beach I had the unnerving experience of looking up to find myself face to face with an iguana hanging down the back of a local man on his way to market to sell the poor beast. In addition to daily meditation practice, discourses from the teacher, and bioenergetics, I learned about reflexology and had my first massage. Lying under the stars at night we practised star bathing with arms and legs outstretched to make a four-pointed star; while sitting in a small circle with hands touching we practised the meditation of dream yoga.

The journey back to Toronto took us seven days as the bus kept breaking down, which meant we were thankfully able to sleep overnight in a bed on two occasions, and spend long enough in Guadalajara to explore and make purchases in a wonderful market there. From the humid heat of Mexico we arrived back in Canada to winter snows.

Home in time for Christmas, I discovered that the cheque I had made out to the travel agent for the fare to Canada was invalid and had not been cashed. This was the reason I had found enough money in my account to cover the cost of the course and the bus fare to and from Mexico! It was another nine months before the travel agent discovered that I still owed them the fare, and by that time I had earned enough to pay them!

In April of 1975 there was a two-week meditation course in southern Scotland at Laurieston Hall, one of the first alternative communities in Britain, and as far as I know still going strong. It was here that the Rinpoche baffled me by repeating the words "Of course Roslyn is so spiritual, sooo spiritual." I was still teaching yoga and taking meditation practice very seriously. Surely I was to be praised for this, not mocked! One day we visited a beach covered in plastic and other rubbish washed up by the sea. We were instructed to clean it up, and by the end of the day we had filled more than fifty black bags. Another day we went to visit an ancient castle that was being offered for sale at the price of £8,000 for a ten-year lease. We were beginning to look for a suitable centre for our newly formed Crystal Group, the name given by the teacher, the purpose of which was to create a group of students to meet on occasions to practise meditation, and provide a venue for Rinpoche to teach in the future. Of course the medieval castle was completely impractical. None of us could imagine living in such a cold, inhospitable, isolated environment.

Crete and Samos

The next adventure with the Rinpoche followed with a three-month retreat in Crete and Samos. I let my flat to two of my friend Joan's girls, and spent three days in the Magic Bus with non-stop Greek music blaring from the loud speakers, travelling down to Athens together with three other members of the Crystal Group. I've never been able to appreciate Greek music since! From there we met up with other students and the teacher, and took a boat from Piraeus to Crete, and a bus to Paleochora in the southwest. We were to camp near the town. As I had no tent I bought a piece of sailcloth in Xania, and with some help made myself an open-sided shelter from the sun in a lemon and carob orchard. I was lucky enough to find an old rusty iron bedstead, which was more comfortable than sleeping on the ground, and which kept me away from the creepy-crawlies. We had a discourse from the Rinpoche each morning in the local hall, and some afternoons at his house, which required his students to labour up the steep slopes of a hill in the blazing sun. One time I arrived in a distressed state with a touch of sunstroke, and had to be revived with cold compresses to the back of my neck before the class. We also had classes in astrophysics, during which time I wrote an essay on black holes, practised sacred dance, and studied astrology, the healing arts, computers and science. I remember rehearsing *Oedipus Rex*, which we subsequently performed. In between classes and rehearsing we had at least two Tibetan deity initiations each week, when we were required to repeat 100,000 mantras within three days. We carried our malas (rosaries) wherever we went, for the purpose of counting. One time we were instructed to spend three days fasting in isolation, with no access to fluids. The idea was to spend our nights in a cave. There were plenty of them up in the hills, but they also housed snakes and wild animals, so I chickened out and found some overhanging rocks on a beach, where I endeavoured to sleep, until the tide came in and soaked my sleeping bag. Except for evening meals at the local restaurant we were expected to be in silence as we practised meditation during our two months in Crete. On our days off I sometimes took a bus across the mountain into Xania, once being fortunate in catching a Mikis Theodorakis concert. Other times I spent swimming in the sea, one of my great loves. All in all this was a very happy time for me.

When the heat became too intense we moved on to Samos. First we returned to the mainland to visit some places of special interest. I was joined by Melanie who had travelled by train to Athens, and David who arrived by plane. We travelled with the dharma group to Corinth, Mycenae and Naplio. At Delphi, the home of the oracle, Rinpoche gave us an order to climb up an almost perpendicular rock to the source of the oracle's voice. I was fortunate to have a helping hand pushing me up from behind! We visited Epidavros, the magnificent amphitheatre, where we watched a production of *Lysistrata*, and then met the Rinpoche there the next morning to view the ruins of the ancient healing centre. This was the Asclepius healing sanctuary, the hospital that used dream yoga and herbs for healing. At the amphitheatre, capable of seating 15,000 people, it was said that a stage whisper could be heard from the very top stone seating area. Of course I had to try it out, together with some Shakespeare, and part of a speech from Shaw's *St Joan*!

The next morning we left for Samos. There was no available accommodation in Agios Konstantinos where we were based, so David and I slept on the ground in our sleeping bags. The classes here were influenced by Pythagoras the mathematician and musician. We visited the capital town Pythagoria, named after him, with its ancient aqueduct. After three weeks sleeping in the open, David and I thankfully moved into a vacant room, as we were beginning to suffer from insect bites and the sound of frogs jumping on and over us. Melanie also developed a serious rash after rolling on the pine-strewn ground while demonstrating some dance. There was the danger of scorpions, which I had experienced in Mexico. One of the Canadian students was so afraid of being bitten that he wrapped himself up from head to toe, just leaving his nose exposed. Of course that is just where he was bitten, and had to be rushed to hospital in a serious condition – an example of how fear attracts!

At the end of the course on Samos some of the students followed the teacher to Pamukkale, a hot-springs resort in nearby Turkey. My money spent, David and I decided to do the return journey via Venice, which I had long wished to visit again. We picked up a boat that plies between Haifa and Venice at the port of Piraeus and arrived in Venice after two nights on this rundown vessel. A couple of nights there, two more with a friend in France, then home, after more than three months away.

Living in Gloucestershire

Within a few days of returning home that September, I had moved out of my flat to live a rural life in the cottage in the Forest of Dean, where I had spent only some weekends and the occasional week's holiday. David gave up his job and joined me with the hope of finding local work. Meanwhile I threw myself into country tasks and activities, such as chopping wood for the open fire, cutting down brambles at the bottom of the terraced garden and planting vines. With the arrival of spring I tried my hand at making jams and wine from rhubarb and hedgerow fruit, becoming involved in the joys of country living.

The following January brought news that the Rinpoche would be arriving at Avonmouth the next day, and would be giving a few days' teachings at my cottage before going on to London. Together with two other students we drove to the docks to meet the boat, the *Zygmunt Stary*, only to be told it wouldn't be docking until the next morning. Back at the cottage we found a number of Rinpoche's students had arrived in an old ambulance, all of whom had to be accommodated in the one living room! At six the next morning we once again left for Avonmouth, this time in a hired car. After boarding the ship and visiting Rinpoche in his cabin, we drove with him back to the Forest of Dean and Speech House, a former ancient courthouse, now a hotel, where I had booked a room with a seventeenth-century four-poster bed. With him standing by, I nervously booked him in giving his original name of George Dawson, as instructed. In the thirty years in which I knew him I never lost my feeling of awe in his presence. He remained a charismatic figure, for me and all his students, until his death in Switzerland in 2004. That evening he gave his first discourse to twenty-three eager students, and I felt happy and proud to be once again hosting a meditation retreat with this great enlightened teacher. He gave two more days of teachings and some advice for me on what to do with my large rocky garden. I then followed him to London for another week's intensive teaching there.

Early that spring I made the acquaintance of a lovely couple who, having trained in psychosynthesis, were now putting it to good use by running self-awareness weekends in their home, White Rocks, at Garway Hill in Herefordshire. After participating in one of their courses I was asked to teach a weekly yoga class. Shortly afterwards I ran my first weekend yoga course at Hawkwood College, a large Victorian course centre outside Stroud. This was the start of a happy relationship in which I was to run weekend and whole-week courses in Hawkwood's beautiful, peaceful environment for the next sixteen years.

Later that spring David started a job at a chicken farm, the only work he could find. He stuck it for a few months until the battery-hen conditions proved too much for him and he packed it in. Meanwhile I was enjoying this simple way of life. I now had plenty of time to read, practise yoga and meditation and explore the Forest, the Wye Valley and river, with the towns of Ross and Monmouth nearby. I began to plan a week's yoga holiday course at Catherine's farmhouse near Cahors in the Lot-et-Garonne department of France, where David and I had stayed on our way back from Samos. I put an advert in *The Times*, and waited for replies. The course would include weaving taught by Catherine, dance by Kate, a former Dartington student friend of Melanie's, and pottery by François, Catherine's youngest son. The organisation proved more difficult than I imagined. After being picked up at the railway station by one of Catherine's sons in a broken-down car, which only just made the journey, I found that nothing had been prepared. Somehow we muddled through with half a dozen students from England, one of whom had to be taken to hospital halfway through the week, while Kate managed to give herself concussion on a low barn beam! Luckily the weather stayed fine, the view was much appreciated, and by the end we had all enjoyed the course.

Staying overnight in Camden Town on my way home

to Gloucestershire, I happened to see a notice in a health-food shop advertising a lecture to be given the following night on the subject of primal integration by Dr William Swartley. I decided to stay on an extra day and attend the lecture. Little did I know that this decision would change the direction of my life. Listening to this Canadian therapist, calling himself a Hindu Buddhist, and declaring that in spite of being an eminent psychiatrist, he knew nothing, I felt drawn to him in a similar way as I had to the Rinpoche when I first heard him talk a few years earlier. He announced he would be giving a four-day workshop at the Churchill Centre near Baker Street, and I felt impelled to join it. My experience in Mexico with primal work had made a deep impression. Bill Swartley's method of primal integration entailed lying on the carpet of the group room in the foetal position with the intention of re-experiencing one's own birth. As everything we have ever experienced is recorded in the body, he maintained that we all have a memory of our birth. With the help of music and an accompanying therapist, the womb becomes a reality, and the inter-uterine experience a familiar state. Finally there is a simulated experience of one's own birth, revealing formerly unknown details, which may have become subsequent life patterns. During the third day of the workshop I relived an aspect of my birth. I was to go through further experiences of my birth on several more occasions. As a newly born infant I remained in the therapy room for the rest of that night, sleeping on the floor surrounded by cushions. The next day I wandered out and into Regent's Park viewing the world in wonder, with new eyes. I found myself meeting and conversing with four separate strangers. Strangely I also met a young woman I knew, who happened to be the daughter of the Canadian primal therapist, a student of Rinpoche's, who had been with me on the course in Mexico! The sense of being very young, open and innocent remained with me for the next few days.

When I finally returned to my cottage I found that the vegetable garden had been decimated by sheep. This was the very hot summer of 1976 and sheep that were allowed to roam freely in the Forest of Dean were now roaming into gardens. Apparently David had woken in the middle of the night to discover them, and had raced out quite naked, shouting and brandishing a broom! Losing all our vegetable plants so carefully tended through our first winter and spring was heart-breaking.

Instead of a quiet country existence, life was beginning to be more and more hectic. As well as weekly classes in Stroud, I was running weekend yoga courses at White Rocks in Herefordshire. After the weekend course at Hawkwood College, together with some of my yoga students that Easter, we visited Brockwood Park to hear Krishnamurti give his famous talks. In the summer Melanie had her twenty-first birthday party at the cottage, with friends coming down from London to sleep in tents on the terraces and on the living-room floor. Two weeks later I drove Melanie back to Dartington where she was to spend her third year at Exmouth Rolle College, taking a BEd degree. I returned to the cottage and on to London, where I was now doing massage training over several weekends.

Primal Integration

Meanwhile I was continuing to explore primal integration with William Swartley at the Churchill Centre, and by November I decided to embark on a two-year primal training course, while finishing off my massage course. On Remembrance Sunday, RD Laing, the well-known psychiatrist, lectured our training group, followed by Frederick Leboyer, founder of the natural birth movement, and Frank Lake, the theologian psychiatrist. He was running primal workshops at that time for members of the clergy and nuns in his hometown of Nottingham.

At the beginning of 1977 David left Lydbrook to study Japanese at the School of Oriental and Asian Studies in London. I was now on my own, and continuing to enjoy living in the country. My nearest neighbour, Mrs Mitchell, had fourteen cats, which all lived in the house together with her seventeen-year-old son, another son aged six and her butcher husband. I avoided entering her house as the smell was overpowering. Her young son Billy used to visit me and I noticed his movements had become slow and deliberate. It was discovered he had developed a brain tumour, and he died suddenly. There was a local rumour that his father had pushed him downstairs precipitating his condition. People living in the Forest of Dean seemed to be fifty years behind the times, as though stuck in a time warp. Because I was known to be practising massage and yoga, I was considered to be a witch!

I continued to run a weekly yoga class near Stroud, and attend fortnightly primal training weekends in London, but by the summer I decided to sell the cottage and move back to London, as from the autumn term I was required to attend weekly theoretical sessions and case-study evenings in addition to the fortnightly residential weekends. Getting access to my flat proved difficult. Joan's daughters wouldn't budge, so I took up the offer of a bed in the laundry room of one of my fellow-students. Finally Bill Swartley, who also needed accommodation, took up my cause, and managed to persuade them to leave. I never found out how! So he and partner Jean moved into a room in the flat, while I was thankful to be back after an absence of two years.

Thus began an intensely exciting period of my life. I was teaching yoga again several days a week, running a weekly massage course and becoming deeply involved with the primal-integration training. I was asked to co-lead a weekend residential group of two five-day intensive workshops at the Churchill Centre, and felt I had arrived! I loved all this diverse teaching and always seemed to have bags of energy. I thought of myself as Superwoman!

In November a bombshell was dropped! We learned that Bill had cancer. After visiting a specialist in his hometown, Toronto, he learned that the tumour was growing steadily, and was inoperable. Jean, his partner, was devastated, as we all were! Meanwhile he continued with the work.

Jack Painter arrived from California to teach us postural integration, and I learned from him the Reichian work that I was to go on to use and teach for many years to come. Stanislav Grof, the noted psychiatrist, researching altered states of consciousness, joined our training group to observe Bill's work with us. He learned that one could experience these states and early trauma without the use of LSD, which he had been working with and writing about.

Meanwhile we studied the four stages of birth from his book *Realms of the Human Unconscious*. In later years he went on to run international workshops extremely successfully, using breathing and music, as Bill had done, calling his method holotropic breathing. That same week His Holiness the Sixteenth Karmapa gave his black hat initiation at the Friends Meeting House in Euston, which Bill and I attended, and where, on taking refuge (seeking protection in the dharma), I was given the Tibetan name of Karma Sonam Drolma. By the end of the year Bill and Jean had moved out of my flat to live in the large house the Churchill Centre were renting for our residential weekends in Caversham.

In 1978 I had begun to work as a reflexologist and masseuse at a naturopathic clinic in Park Street, Mayfair, three days a week, run by Joseph Goodman, a well-known acupuncturist and osteopath, whom I had known as an actor in Johannesburg, and who played opposite me as Romeo when we represented South Africa in the Cavalcade of Commonwealth. Meanwhile I continued to teach five yoga classes a week. At an Association of Humanistic Psychology conference I ran my first primal workshop at West Dean College in Sussex. In addition to the massage course I had run with Jack Painter at the Churchill Centre I began to give massage workshops in Bath, at a Buddhist community in Kent, and classes privately at home in London. I continued to attend the fortnightly primal residential weekends with a series of international therapists, including the Americans Cecil Burney, a Jungian using sand-tray work, Ed Elkin, the Gestalt therapist, Michael Broder and Paco, the principal of the Reichian Institute in Mexico City. During one weekend I had what appeared to be a past-life experience. Working with a colleague, using regression techniques, I found myself dragging along the floor with a damaged right leg, and in great pain, while all around me was gunfire and explosions. I thought I had reached a barbed-wire fence, when there was a great flash of light and then blackness. I believed I had been a soldier killed on the battlefields of France during the First World War. The experience left me quite shaken.

In July that year I gave a lecture on primal integration at Leamington Spa Health Festival, and later that week ran a workshop at a health and healing conference in Loughborough. In the summer, Penny Nield-Smith, my old yoga teacher, joined me to teach on a week-long yoga course at Hawkwood College, together with Kofi Busia, a well-known Nigerian yoga teacher from Oxford who worked with the more advanced students. A week later I was running my first residential humanistic personal development workshop in Herefordshire. I invited John Rowan, a leading figure in the humanistic psychology movement, to join me as co-facilitator for the week, which didn't prove entirely successful. He disliked being in the country, and I disliked his aggressive encounter style with the group, giving rise to some disagreement. However I loved all this diverse teaching and my energy seemed to be endless. A few days later David and I took off for a few days in the Lake District at Buttermere, on our way to a rented cottage in Scotland for a week on Loch Torridon in Wester Ross. In spite of it being summer the weather proved cold and wet!

Later that year I visited Bill Swartley in a flat in Maida Vale and found him in a good deal of pain with his advanced cancer. I had waited half an hour on the steps outside the front door for him to answer the doorbell. He told me the only relief he could find was soaking in a hot bath. This was a very poignant time as I knew it would be the last time I would see him. I was leaving for India the following week to study with yoga teacher, BKS Iyengar. Bill was a lovely man, and I had grown very fond of him.

India

So off to India for three months together with a group of yoga teachers from the north of England, only a couple of whom I knew. Arriving in Bombay we transferred to taxis for the ride to Poona where Mr Iyengar had his well-known teaching ashram. The wrecks of vehicles along the side of the road and chaotic driving conditions certainly didn't inspire one with confidence, and I was relieved to arrive in Poona, a few hours later, in one piece. I was taken to a guesthouse to prepare for class the next day. The next three weeks were physically the toughest in my experience. I found myself being pushed into positions I never thought possible; being extended beyond what I thought were my capabilities. There would be two or three classes a day for asanas (positions) and pranayama (breathing). As yoga asanas, seemingly working on the body to become more flexible, are also at the same time influencing one's mental, emotional and spiritual aspects, I was being prepared for what I was to experience in the future, and learning how to deal with a more flexible and expanded life. This was Iyengar's sixtieth birthday, a special time when a Brahman renounces family life and embraces the spiritual life. After three weeks of continuous hard work, we participated in a week of sacred rituals with four priests chanting, and a day of feasting in Bombay, and other general celebrations. During one of our Sundays off I took advantage of the chance to visit Bhagwan Rajneesh at his ashram in Poona, where after making a dramatic arrival in one of his luxury vehicles, he gave a talk in English to an adoring audience. I was aware of how seductive was his voice and style of delivery, but refused to be seduced.

I had been preparing for the next stage of my journey in India. Some of the yoga students were staying with a group of nuns in Poona, where I was invited for tea. They told me about Father Bede Griffiths' ashram in the south of the country. I was excited to meet him after having seen a television programme about him a few months earlier. After writing to ask if I could spend Christmas and New Year at the ashram, and receiving a reply in his own hand, welcoming me, I braved the queues of the railway station to book a seat on a train going first to Bangalore, to visit the guru Sai Baba, and to stay with a friend of a yoga student of mine who ran a guesthouse there. While waiting in the railway queue I began talking to a Swiss girl working for the United Nations office in Geneva, who spent three months each year at Kovalam Beach in Kerala in the southwest of the country. She persuaded me to meet her there after visiting the ashram at Shantivanam.

My arrival at Bangalore was quite dramatic. Mrs Gandhi, the prime minister at that time, had just been arrested, and there were protest riots taking place. I managed to reach the guesthouse safely, and was shown to a room outside in the yard, where I was instructed to stay put and not leave if I valued my life! For the next few hours I could hear shouts and found stones raining down on the tin roof of my room. It was a frightening experience. Although hungry, I had to wait till the next day to venture out. I visited Sai Baba's ashram, and after waiting several hours to meet him, he passed me on his way to Madras, waving his hand in greeting like the Queen Mother used to do. The next morning I left Bangalore for Bede Griffiths' ashram, with hours of delays on the railway line while stones were cleared, before arriving at Shantivanam, set on the mighty Cauvery River in Tamil Nadu. Spending Christmas at a Christian Hindu centre was like no other Christmas I'd experienced before. There was the mixed church/temple experience, followed by the usual open-air dinner seated on the ground with a banana leaf for a plate and rice and vegetables sambar, but with an added treat of a shared piece of "plum pudding"! I loved the simplicity of it all. During my very happy stay, I was granted the opportunity of a private discussion with Father Bede, recognised as a great mystic and writer, in his humble hut, consisting of a bed, a table and couple of chairs. Before leaving on New Year's Day I was approached by

Rupert Sheldrake, the biologist, who had been living there for the past two years, who asked me if I could take the manuscript of the book he had been working on back to England with me to have it typed. He assured me that this book, his first, entitled *The Science of Life*, would cause a sensation in the scientific world as he had introduced the concept of God in his work. As it turned out, on my leaving it was not quite finished, but two years later, when I read the reviews, I discovered he had been right about its reception.

I was now on my way by buses and train to Trivandrum and onto Kovalam Beach to meet up with Nichole, the Swiss girl, although I had no address to refer to. The day after my arrival I fortunately met her walking along the idyllic beach, and was able to move into her beach hut with her. During my ten-day stay I travelled down to the southernmost tip of India, where I got caught up in a pilgrimage and religious ceremony at a temple on an island out in the sea, and watched a magnificent sunset with thousands of worshippers – an unforgettable experience! During this time, I learned of the difficult time people were having in a frozen Britain, with strikes affecting the distribution of food, and decided I couldn't stay sunning myself on a beach while people at home were suffering. I decided to cut short my stay in India and made arrangements to get back to Bangalore where I could fly to Bombay and on to London. Staying overnight back at the Regent Guest

House, unfortunately I was violently ill after eating chicken for the first time in India, a foolish mistake, and arrived at Bombay Airport rather the worse for wear!

I took my place in a queue in the hope of getting a seat on a plane back to London as soon as possible. The person in front of me dressed in khaki shorts turned out to be a British archaeologist, and we both found flights available the next day. He was planning to join a dig in central Africa. Together, we inquired about a nearby hotel, as we would need to stay overnight. We made our way there, and at the reception desk I realised I hadn't enough money left to pay for a room. He kindly offered to share his room. I was reassured there would be a couch I could use. It seemed a perfectly good arrangement, and I leapt at the offer. I had no luggage with me, so after he had settled in we went off together to look for presents in the nearby market for me to take home, and then on to a restaurant for dinner. By this time we were walking hand in hand, and seemed to be getting on surprisingly well. It seemed to be turning into a romantic evening! Later, after returning to our room, I had a shower and walked back dressed only in the long white shirt I had been wearing all day, as a makeshift nightdress, displaying a good deal of leg, which seemed to turn him on, while I was finding this good-looking young Englishman quite attractive. Needless to say the couch remained unused! The next morning, at 6.15, my companion accompanied me to the airport, though his plane was not due to leave until much later. When I discovered my plane was delayed until late afternoon, Peter decided to change his plans and fly with me to London. So with time to spare we returned to the hotel to avail ourselves of the use of the swimming pool.

We finally left Bombay at 6.30 that evening. As the plane took off I was startled to hear two distinct bangs below us. No one else seemed to notice, and it was only when we came to land in Rome, where we were due to refuel after circling round the magically lit city for some time, and touched down on the runway with an alarming screech of breaks, that we realised something was seriously wrong. What I had heard on take-off was the sound of two of the tyres bursting, making a normal landing impossible. It's possible that the pilot was preparing for an emergency landing by spending time circling the city to use up the remaining fuel. Together with our fellow-passengers we filed into the airport to await another plane from London. I was thrilled to be so unexpectedly back in my beloved Italy, albeit in Rome in the middle of the night. Peter and I had found a carpeted corner where we attempted to get some sleep, when there was an announcement that we would be taken to a hotel for what remained of the night. So my new friend and I were being given a second night together! Meanwhile, sometime in the early hours Peter had an asthma attack, and I spent time giving him a reflexology treatment to alleviate it. We didn't leave Rome till three o'clock that afternoon, finally arriving at Heathrow at six p.m., where

Peter was met by his fiancée before we had a chance to say goodbye. As a postscript, we did arrange to meet again on a wet and windy day a few weeks later at a restaurant in South Kensington, but the magic had evaporated with the rain, and we knew without words that the excitement of our aircraft romance had died a natural death in the light of everyday life!

Three weeks after returning I learned that Bill Swartley, my beloved primal-integration trainer, and friend had died in Toronto. Six days later a wake was arranged at the Churchill Centre where our training had taken place. There was a solemn ceremony with many candles in a darkened room where we meditated and spent time recalling memories of our experiences with Bill. In the middle of this event I was called away to the office, where I was asked if I would go straight away to a hotel in Kensington to give a massage to the singer Van Morrison, who was in London to give a performance! I was thrown into confusion by this request at such a time. I didn't want to leave the ceremony suddenly, but on the other hand this was a wonderful opportunity to meet the famous singer, whose records I played, and admired. I decided to go, grabbed some massage oil, and took a taxi to the hotel. It turned out to be a bizarre experience. I had no massage table so arranged a place on the floor. Dressed unsuitably in a silk taffeta dress with a wide skirt I decided to take it off and work in my underwear. I had to work hard as the famous man had muscles like steel and remained very tense (possibly he wasn't that comfortable lying on the floor)! While getting dressed he suggested I might like to join him on tour as his masseuse, which I gracefully declined. He offered me tickets for his forthcoming concert, which I also declined, saying that I already had tickets. It didn't occur to me that there were friends who would have loved to have them! He then asked me what was my fee, and I naively asked for £10 to cover the cost of my taxi!

Search for a Centre

About this time I had begun to look at the possibilities of living communally, preferably in a spiritually based community. In March I took a train to Totnes in Devon to visit a Rajneesh community, the Mill House at Gara Bridge, which was up for sale. This beautiful property was set in several acres of bluebell-covered woodland, with a rushing stream and millwheel. I stayed the night with the occupants, members of a Rajneesh community joining them in an outrageous party, and returned to London with a quest to raise £26,000 to buy the property. I had little time to think about the project as I was now preparing for a visit from my teacher, Namgyal Rinpoche, to give a ten-day retreat at my flat. Meanwhile I had already committed myself to an all-day training in Kirlian photography, to take place on a stand at the forthcoming Body, Mind and Spirit Festival at Earls Court. Together with intense teachings each morning and meditation exercises to practise each day, I managed to continue with my yoga classes, my work as a practitioner at the Park Street Clinic in Mayfair and also now in Hendon, run a weekly therapy group at the Open

Centre in the City, and on one day serve lunch to the Rinpoche and the students! On one occasion I visited him in his hotel in Richmond, and during a walk along the Thames I talked about my aspirations to create a community. He warned me of the interpersonal difficulties that arose from living within a community.

Three days later I was running another weekend yoga course at Hawkwood College, and from Stroud I travelled to Seaton in East Devon to meet Paul Zeal of the Philadelphia Association, originally set up by the psychiatrist RD Laing. I was still looking for a large community house, and the association had such a house, St Dympna's, which they wanted to continue to be run as a therapeutic centre. I realised pretty quickly that it wasn't for me. I would have to take on Mary Barnes, a well-known figure in the mental-health world, who would continue to live there. She had famously written a book about her experience of madness, and her experience with the association. Later there was a play about her produced at the Royal Court Theatre. I returned to London in time to take my place on the Kirlian photography stand at the Earls Court Festival for the next week, after which I drove down to East Sussex, to a convent to do a ten-day meditation course with Cecilie, with whom I had stayed in Toronto in 1974. As one of Rinpoche's early students she was already proving herself a fine teacher.

In August I was thrilled to see Martha Graham, the

famous American dancer, dressed in a long flowing black robe, perform her unique method of strong barefoot dance at the Royal Opera House. Although now a great age, her commitment to dance was an inspiration.

Having advertised for people to join me in setting up a therapeutic/healing community, and receiving a good response, I arranged a weekend in the country residence of one of the participants. I had been meeting up with a number of others interested in this project, but there was a shortage of offers of financial contributions. I was prepared to sell my flat but there was only one other person so far prepared to contribute. I had continued to look at suitable venues in different parts of the country, but the possibility of raising the money to buy such a house was proving pretty remote. The following week, after running another yoga course at Hawkwood, I set off for Scotland to take part in Findhorn's Experience Week. I hoped that my time there would help clarify the direction of the next phase of my life. That guidance came from an art therapist during an art exercise. While drawing I had raised the question of where I should move to, and the picture of whirling colours that I produced was interpreted by the teacher as a place of energetic power, such as Glastonbury. Two months earlier I had attended a Wrekin Trust lecture on the summer solstice at Glastonbury. I was told of a former Findhorn member living near Glastonbury, soon to be moving to the States with her American partner, who was looking for a tenant for her cottage. After several failed attempts to phone her, I finally made contact on my last night at Findhorn. "Until yesterday we thought we had a tenant, but she has now backed out," she told me. "Come down and see it as soon as you can." I was due to go on to Laurieston Hall where the community were holding a conference on alternative medicine, and I had been asked to run a couple of workshops. I had previously stayed at Laurieston during a retreat with the Rinpoche in 1975. At the close of the conference I hitched a ride to Dumfries, where after three changes of train I reached Bristol. From there I took a bus to Wells and Shepton Mallet, to be met by Sierra, whom I immediately liked.

The stone cottage at Evercreech was as ancient as the church it faced – possibly fifteenth century. There was an attractive garden with a vegetable plot formed in a semicircle based on the Findhorn model. With the cottage went four cats, which was to prove a bit of a problem. Five weeks later I had moved in. After one night in the master bedroom I was forced to move out again, at least into another room, as the four-poster had been treated with insecticide, which laid me low for several days. I spent very little time at the cottage during the next few weeks, with the cats that were used to human company becoming quite feral. Coming in late at night I had to watch out for offerings of small birds and mice! I had managed to set up a regular yoga class in nearby Glastonbury, and one in Bristol, also continuing to work one day a week at the naturopathic clinic in London, while staying on to visit friends or run a workshop at the weekends. One time, when I had been away for a few days, I returned to find that the kitchen boiler, which Sue, my neighbour, kept stoked during the cold weather, had exploded! It had brought down part of the ceiling in my bedroom, covering the furniture in debris. There was another accident on Christmas Day when a bottle of lemonade exploded scattering glass into the prepared dinner!

After Christmas I prepared to leave for Holland. While at Findhorn I had met Pam, Melanie's old friend who lived and taught clowning in Holland. On arriving in England she had tried to contact me in London, and to her surprise found me in Findhorn. She had that day decided to return to Findhorn in January for a six-week course. Would I consider taking over her classes? Although I hadn't taught mime for at least eight years I agreed to her request. I had explained to Sierra when I first took the cottage that I would be away for all of January and part of February, and she agreed to take possession of her house during that time.

Melanie on her
twenty-first
birthday, at the
cottage in
Lydbrook,
Forest of Dean,
1976

Melanie in Wales, 1978

PART FOUR
1980–1989

The Therapist

*Inner and Outer
Exploration*

Holland

Travelling overnight to Amsterdam I made my way to Pam's room in the red-light district of the city, first by taxi, and finally with a young man on a bicycle helping me carry my suitcase after I was dropped at the wrong address. Pam's room turned out to be situated over a dry-cleaning shop, which couldn't have been too healthy for her. She had left me a list of teaching venues, and that afternoon I followed her directions to the Studio Centre in Amsterdam. The following day I took a train to Eindhoven to attend a festival at the Efenaar Centre. This was a centre concerned with the promotion of New Age, spiritual and cultural events. On the way I stopped off at Den Bosch to examine the teaching venue there. During a long weekend at the Efenaar Centre I managed to attend lectures and videos on evolution, with Alan Watts on Zen, and Alexander Lowen on Bioenergetics. Pam arrived to give a workshop on sensory awareness, and after she left the following day I made my way to Den Bosch to give the first of my two classes – on reflexology, and that evening on mime and improvisation. After a day off, I was in Rotterdam to give a three-hour class and stay the night with Marianne and her daughters. Marianne subsequently became a good friend. At the end of that week I was back at the Efenaar Centre to run my own workshop, introducing trust exercises, bioenergetics, massage and dance.

At the end of the following week, after my class in Rotterdam I took a train to Hanover in Germany, where I had arranged to run a weekend bioenergetics therapy workshop. I had been invited by Anne who ran a yoga studio in the city. She was delighted to find someone who worked with both practices. Bioenergetics, based on Wilhelm Reich's work, which aims to relieve emotional blocks in the body, is quite a different approach from yoga practice, but they both aim to restore the individual to a balanced state. On the train journey I loved the sight of skaters in multi-hued clothes on the lakes we passed, reminding me of the time in repertory at Ipswich when I first experienced skating in the open on a flooded iced-over field.

At the end of my six weeks teaching in Holland I took a train to Paris to stay with David, who was now working there. I had enjoyed my time in Holland. The students were enthusiastic and friendly. They were eager to learn anything I offered, and I was glad to be given overnight accommodation when I needed it. I found travelling around the country easy and safe, and it was fascinating staying in the red-light district, where prostitutes, sitting in display windows, openly offered their wares! It was good to see David again, and when he had some free time during the next few days we did the tourist sites, while I was able to fit in a couple of yoga classes with a well-known French Iyengar yoga teacher.

On arriving back in Somerset I found to my dismay that a friend of Sierra's, with her husband and two children, and her nine cats, had moved into my home. What's more, I learned they were there to stay, and I was expected to move out and find alternative accommodation as soon as possible. Although there had been an understanding with Sierra, who owned the house, that I would be away from it for six weeks, there was nothing in writing, and not having her address in the States where I could contact her, it seemed there was nothing I could do about it. I duly began a search for accommodation in Glastonbury, Bristol and Bath, while continuing with my Friday work at the clinic in London. Finally I decided to move back to my flat in London.

I was now working two days a week at the clinic in Mayfair, and seeing private clients at home for massage, reflexology and psychotherapy, while teaching yoga in the evenings for the Inner London Education Authority, and in the summer running a week-long course at Hawkwood. There were two wonderful weeks in Greece at the Skyros Growth Centre, where I threw myself into one week of dance therapy with Masha from the University of New York, and a week of Gestalt with a French therapist, with whom I fell out after the first few days. He sensed I was critical of his work, and he turned abusive, so I took myself off to the beach for the remainder of the week. We could bathe nude from that beach, and I still have photographs of a group of us presenting our bare bodies fore and aft! High up a hill I discovered a very special monument to the memory of Rupert Brooke, who had died on the island during the First World War. As a teenager I had slept with a copy of his poems and his photographs under my pillow at night.

On my return home I began to run what would become regular personal development growth weekend workshops in Somerset at a beautiful old stone house in Butleigh, near Glastonbury. The theme of the workshop tended to reflect where I was in my own life, and my needs, so the first theme, Becoming Whole, was integrating Jung's four factors – thinking, feeling sensing and intuition – by using exercises I had been introduced to in classes with the Rinpoche. During the course of the workshop I would introduce exercises to bring these aspects of ourselves together through the effective tools of movement, visualisation, psychodrama, bioenergetics, Gestalt, primal integration and the use of touch. At this time I was passionate about the development of the human potential. I wanted to enable people to find their true selves, to connect with their intrinsic nature. I have always believed we can achieve what we aim for, and more, when we cease to limit ourselves. The form of Reichian deep breathing and massage I used in these workshops, and continued to use for many years in weekend workshops and with individual clients, could produce an altered state of consciousness, where aspects of the unconscious could be brought into consciousness through access to deep early memories, and occasionally presenting what appeared to be past-life experiences. I found this an effective tool for resolving and healing what continued to be problematic and disturbing areas of people's lives. At a later time, when I found myself having to make new decisions in my own life, the workshop was entitled Turning Point, or when arriving at a crossroads in my life. Then there was Surrender to the Unknown, when learning to let go and trust to the universe; and Nurturing Ourselves, when needing to do so more and more in my busy life.

Namgyal Rinpoche was back in England and I managed once again to attend his discourses, which were always inspirational, leaving me with a sense of well-being and a belief that anything was possible. This took place in a student's lovely mill house in Surrey, followed by a week of meditation with Cecilie, his senior student, at a Catholic retreat centre near Slough. By now I had begun my own therapy with a well-known Jungian therapist, Carol Jeffreys. During my initial interview I had expressed my anxiety that at the age of eighty-two she might die, as my group therapist Bill Swartley had done. She assured me she had no intention of going until well into her nineties! Sure enough, some ten years later,

I met her again in Totnes where she had been invited to give a talk to some psychotherapists!

By the end of the year I returned to Holland to run several workshops, then on to Hanover to run another weekend bioenergetics psychotherapy workshop. When I look back at my life during the 1980s, the image of me that comes to mind is that of a butterfly newly out of its chrysalis. I was running my first workshops in Europe, making new friends and also introducing them to healing methods of massage, reflexology and body therapies. I had always loved travelling, and here I was being paid to travel and work at what I enjoyed. I have always felt that my life is about enabling people to recognise their potential, develop their awareness and creativity, and continue to grow.

David was now living permanently in Paris teaching English. Although we had spent very little time together during the previous few years, I felt surprisingly bereft by his departure. Ours had been a strange relationship, probably based on a mutual need for companionship. I paid him another visit in Vincennes, where he was living, and returned to London in time to get the cheap alternative Magic Bus trip to Hamburg, on the first lap of a journey to South America.

Journey to South America

Previously I had asked the Rinpoche if I could travel with him on one of his journeys, this time to South America, and he had accepted me. I would be one of ten students on a cargo boat leaving from Hamburg taking twelve passengers only, with him and his attendant making up the full quota. This would be a unique opportunity of inner and outer exploration, a physical interpretation of the meaning of the dharma as an exploration of the laws of life. With no specific information about when we were likely to embark, Margaret, a former casting director at Granada Television, and myself, arrived in Hamburg and booked into the St George's Hotel to await instruction. I spent the next few days visiting museums and galleries including a fine Tutankhamen exhibition. A week later a call came to go to shed 84/85 where we would find the Polish Ocean Lines freighter *Heweliusz*, and be joined by the teacher and his attendant, Terry. Once on board, the ten students, made up of five Canadians, three Swiss and the two of us from England, were allocated a simple cabin with two sharing, and a primitive shower. The passenger lounge would be our teaching space. We would meet with the captain and officers at mealtimes only. There was an immediate problem when a couple of officers propositioned me and a young Swiss woman to meet with them socially. They were understandably angry when we politely refused. We were unable to explain that we were there on a meditation course!

From day one I found myself having a problem with the food. Polish food consisted predominantly of meat for breakfast, lunch and dinner, accompanied by potatoes or rice. As a practising vegetarian since 1972, I had been warned to prepare myself for a change of diet. Thus I made an effort to eat a little meat at dinner at least. The most difficult time came when, seated at the teacher's table, he passed on some of his meat portion to me. It wasn't easy to appreciate his action as a desire to break my long-term habit and fixed view about food!

After a couple of days getting accustomed to our sea legs, we commenced classes. There were generally three a day – the morning class based on purification of mind, the afternoon on purification of speech and the evening class on purification of body. Between classes we practised meditation exercises, studied, worked on anatomical drawings and mandalas. We also sunned ourselves, enjoyed marine life; scanning the sea for dolphins and whales, and experienced the ocean's variety of moods. There was much to view, from glorious sunsets to fantastic displays of stars, which we studied with binoculars at night. For exercise I was asked to supervise individual yoga practice each morning, and I took to running regularly every day round and round the outer perimeter of the deck. As the central area was covered with cars and trucks, lashed together with ropes, that was a no-go area. As long as the sea was calm this was a great way to live and meditate. However when the weather was rough, the boat being without stabiliser – that was when I longed for dry land.

After thirteen days crossing the Atlantic and passing through the Saragossa Sea and its strange acres of floating algae, we finally arrived in South America. We sailed into the harbour at Maracaibo in Venezuela, and waited for permission to dock. There we languished for eight extremely hot days in view of several oil rigs and a magnificent long bridge. With the crew becoming restless at not being able to go ashore, some small crafts arrived with prostitutes to serve the men. Finally we were given permission to land, and for the next few days we were able to go on exploratory trips. Next we left for Barranquilla in Colombia, where we stayed for a week. Apart from a depressing visit to the local zoo, where the animals looked ill and badly treated, I remember nothing more of that town. Our next port of call was Cartagena, an old Spanish town sporting a magnificent fort. At each port, items were unloaded and others taken on board. The best thing for me was the appearance of fresh vegetables. Rinpoche instructed us to look for unusual fruits, which we divided and sampled after dinner in the evenings. While in Cartagena I was accompanied by a ship's officer to a dentist he knew. I had recently been suffering with toothache, but on examination the dentist concluded that the unaccustomed meat I was eating was the cause, and complimented me on the fine condition of my teeth! On arrival at the dentist's house I was reminded of my native South Africa, with the padlocked fence, barred windows and heavily locked front door. While in Columbia we were warned to stick together, not to wear rings, wristwatches or sunglasses, and to hide any handbags or purses. It was considered then the most dangerous country in the world, where even the police were suspect, so it was no use reporting a crime.

At the next port of call, San Cristóbal, I bought a duty-free penknife, which I still use. About this time I reported certain meditation experiences I was having, which resulted in my being instructed to remain confined to the ship instead of being able to go ashore again. This was to enable me to go more deeply into what now appeared to be the experience of the first stage of birth. I was to put pressure on the front of my head while lying in a cramped space. I was of course familiar with this work from my primal training, and subsequent work with clients. I felt miserable and resentful at not being out enjoying myself with the other students. A few days later we left San Cristóbal, the port for the Panama City, which we could see in the distance, and began the approach to the great canal. It took thousands of prisoners several years to build this series of canals linking two large lakes.

The boat passed infinitely slowly through the first very narrow canal, drawn along by a tugboat on either side, until the canal opened into the first lake. We were able to appreciate the tropical beauty of the scenery as it was still light, but our group continued to stay up through much of the night so as not to miss the event. In the morning we finally woke to a grey Pacific Ocean. It hadn't escaped my notice that passing through the Panama Canal was reflecting my own birth process, even to the eight-hour duration of the journey, matching the timing of my birth. For the next few days we were on silent retreat as we made our way down the west coast of South America. I was now sharing my cabin with Cecilie. Experiencing myself as a new-born at this time, in need of nurturing, her silence felt like the cold indifference of a mother. While added to the now cold weather and fog, my life felt unbearable. Later I was able to appreciate the fact that I was living the post-natal experience with my own unloving mother.

Peru

Five days later, with little to see of the coastline for fog, we approached Peru. Looking down into the water from the deck of the ship as we drew into the harbour in Lima I was delighted to see a mass of red, orange and purple jelly fish, nothing like the thinly coloured ones washed up on our English shore. Lima held the surviving gold treasures of the Incas, but also massive open rubbish heaps where children raked about for food and the hope of hidden treasure. I revelled in the variety of fruit and vegetables obtainable, including my favourite, avocado pears. On one occasion, while buying fruit from a market stall, I was passed a note from the woman stallholder warning me to watch out. She must have observed someone with their eye on my purse. We visited a few museums, including the wonderful Gold Museum with the Rinpoche, who was always instructive. Whenever we docked at a port all formal teachings ceased, but we continued to live on the boat. From Lima we moved down the coast to another Peruvian port, Matarani, where I planned to disembark. The boat was continuing on to Chile, which I had no wish to visit in view of its notorious government at that time. Leaving with me were a Swiss couple and two Canadians, and although the rest of the students and teacher would continue on the boat, ultimately returning to Europe, I had decided to stay in Peru for a few weeks and then fly back to the UK.

Travelling by taxi through a desert of yellow, pink and purple sand we arrived at the charming whitewashed town of Arequipa, some 6,000 feet up, nestling beneath snow-capped mountains. The Rinpoche joined us that day, and the next day I booked a ticket on a train going to Cuzco. A Canadian girl I was with decided to fly home, so I was on my own.

As the train climbed higher and higher I was offered some coca by one of the Peruvians in my coach, against altitude sickness. Another woman trying to befriend me warned me against some of the people in the coach she knew. After a whole day on the train we arrived at eight p.m. at Cuzco Station. Here this same woman insisted on my sharing a taxi with her and some men friends. She wanted me to go to her lodgings with her, and although I had not booked any accommodation I asked the taxi driver to take me to the address of a guesthouse I had found in a guidebook, run by an American who offered trips into the rainforest. I definitely didn't trust her. I left my fellow-travellers with relief and prayed I would be offered a room, but no, they were full that night. There would be a room available the next day. Fortunately they took pity on me, as it was getting very late and I had nowhere to go, and let me stay overnight in a cubbyhole under the stairs, where I wondered whose were the shoes under the bed! After a few days of acclimatising myself to the altitude of 14,000 feet, I inquired about a trip to the rainforest. Bob, the American who ran the guesthouse, and formerly a tourist guide (now retired), assured me that if I could make up a small group he would be willing to take us. There was a young American couple staying at the guesthouse with whom I had already done a trip to Machu Picchu, taking the local dawn train to that magical site and returning the same evening. (While there I had had a strong feeling of *déjà vu*, and I learned later that bones found in the graveyard were mainly female, thought to have been those of priestesses living in that sacred place.) They were also keen to go to the rainforest, and Bob's nephew agreed to join us, so we were now a group and ready to go!

We set off in an ancient truck, spending the first night in an Indian village before climbing up into the Andes, where at 16,000 feet, on getting out of the vehicle, I found it really difficult to walk. As we dropped down through tropical vegetation we passed some impressive waterfalls, and at one point we were forced to stop to admire a myriad of yellow and blue butterflies sunning themselves on the road. Later we came to areas that had been cleared for growing soya, an example of forest clearing, including logging, which I had known about and deplored. Finally we arrived at the Madre de Dios River, where we transferred to a dinghy that we helped to pump up. We planned to paddle down the river to Erica, where Bob had arranged for us to stay with friends he had contacted by radio. Messages could be conveyed before eight o'clock in the morning, this being the only form of communication in that area. We had been going for about twenty minutes when we stopped at the riverbank to pick up a man who needed a lift home. On arrival at his hacienda he invited us to lunch. Walking through his plantation Bob pointed out coffee and coco plants. After a lunch of tortilla and salad it was tempting to remain relaxing in the shade of his veranda, but we had to get on in order to arrive before dark. A level of excitement ensued when we found ourselves having to negotiate some rapids. "Paddle like mad," was the instruction, and with eyes tight shut with fear I did my best to obey. We finally arrived at our destination as light began to fade and we were met by our host, his wife and baby. We were shown to separate thatched wooden huts before sitting down to a meal of freshly caught fish and home-grown vegetables.

Armed with machetes we set off the first morning to explore the forest. I hoped we might come across a remote Indian village, or at least find some indigenous animals, but all we heard and saw were monkeys swinging high up in the trees. On the third day of our stay we left the young family in our dinghy and continued downstream to meet up with our truck on the opposite shore. Returning to Cuzco I arranged for a flight home –

initially flying terrifyingly between mountains in a local plane to Lima, and after spending a night there, on to Miami, and finally after three months away back to London. On describing my recent experiences to a friend, and mentioning the excitement of shooting rapids on the river, she misunderstood me, exclaiming "But I thought you were a vegetarian!" After arriving home I found myself in a good deal of pain from an anal fissure caused by my unusual diet of meat, and after enduring it for several months I finally went into hospital for an operation.

Further
Psychotherapy Training

At the beginning of 1982 I began three years of training in social psychiatry and clinical psychotherapy, after being persuaded by a friend that our careers demanded such an orthodox course. The first year consisted of weekly seminars and group therapy at Dr Joshua Bierer's consulting rooms in Harley Street. Dr Bierer was a colourful octogenarian Adlerian still in practice. Life was now taken up at weekends with regular workshops for BASP (British Association of Social Psychiatry), attending Crystal Group meetings, and visiting Melanie at the Cardiff Laboratory Theatre in Wales, where she was working. One of our Crystal Group members had begun to build a canal narrow boat, and any free weekend was spent painting and furnishing it once it was finished. We painted it in traditional Tibetan Buddhist designs and colours, and when finally launched, the boat, named *Crystal Arc*, drew admiring comments from the occupants of other narrow boats we passed on the canal. The day finally arrived when our teacher gave a course on the boat near Tring, with students sitting two-by-two down its length! When Melanie arrived during that time to pay him a visit, he asked her if she had chosen dharma or drama to pursue in her life, and not surprisingly her reply was the latter.

That summer I attended a week's international conference of the Association of Humanistic Psychology in Paris where I was offering a workshop, and where I had an unforeseen experience. Once again I stayed with David, and as usual we shared a bed. However this time he insisted on placing a dividing bolster down the centre of the bed. I was so upset by this that when the following evening I was invited out for dinner by an American Gestalt therapist, I took up his offer of accommodation in his apartment that night. I didn't return to David's flat till late the next day, to find a very worried man who had left messages for me at the conference centre. He admitted being in love with a young French girl he had met, while I, feeling totally rejected, continued to live it up, with evenings dining out and staying with my new American friend.

After the conference two friends arrived to take me for a holiday in the Cévennes area of France. Our accommodation was in the most beautiful converted barn at Mas de la Carrière, set among mountains with a blessed river where we could cool down in the very hot weather. I was delighted to find the Roy Hart Theatre nearby that my old friend Roy had set up many years before. Sadly he and his wife were killed in a car accident a year or two earlier. However the theatre training was continuing with trusted teachers, and one evening I managed to see a performance by Enrico of Eugenio Barba's Danish *Odin Teatret.*

In November that year I was excited to find myself working with some teachers from Grotowski's Polish physical-based theatre at the Chapter Centre in Cardiff. It proved to be one of the most intense experiences over a period of six days, when we were expected to move, together with the making of sounds, for a period of five hours at a specifically arranged time during the day or night. Apart from one pee break the movement work was nonstop! I found the experience inspiring and memorable. I had long wished to work with Grotowski himself but never found the time to get to Poland.

At the beginning of 1983 my clinical psychotherapy training moved to Guy's Hospital with lectures and practical work with patients two days a week there, and another day at a day centre. When I arrived at the office of the consultant psychiatrist to whom I had been assigned I greeted him cheerily with "I have been relegated to you." The look on his face told me I had chosen the wrong word! In spite of this unfortunate introduction, I later found myself teaching a yoga class to the teenage patients in his department. He had been attending a yoga class, and found it beneficial for himself. I continued with my general yoga teaching, my personal-growth weekend workshops in Somerset, and seeing private clients at home. During this time I became interested in the psychological approach to cancer. I attended a lecture by Carl Simonton at the Royal Society of Medicine, on his individual approach, and worked with a group of patients at the Royal Marsden Hospital.

Return to South Africa

In August that year I flew to South Africa to visit my parents. I had not been back to the country since the year Michael died twenty-four years earlier. I was happy to stay with my old friend Jo, whom I have loved all my life, and my dear old drama mentor and teacher Norah Taylor. Not much had changed since my last visit. Apartheid still ruled with a firm hand. A highlight of my stay was arranging to visit Dennis, my first boyfriend, whom I hadn't met for thirty years since he came to visit me in London. I had first been introduced to him in Johannesburg by Margaret, a fellow-budding actress. I was seventeen and Dennis was a couple of years older and studying at the Witwatersrand University. He would take me out to dinner or dancing, and I would see more of him when staying with my aunt and uncle in Pretoria, where his family lived. I knew his father was a millionaire. However our friendship cooled after he found me being kissed by his friend Costa on the veranda of a clubhouse dance one night, and shortly after I left for England. He now owned a vast citrus estate in the northern Transvaal. The overnight train from Johannesburg arrived at six a.m., and I woke to hear him calling my name as the train arrived at the station. The main house was set in a beautiful cultivated garden leading down to a lake. After one failed marriage he had married Margaret, who spent her time cultivating orchids, and was now away on holiday. The next few days were emotionally charged, and quite magical. I was given my own suite of rooms in a separate building on the estate, swam each morning in the nearby pool, was taken to visit a cave with prehistoric cave paintings on Dennis's estate, and shown over his African village, where schoolchildren sang to us beautifully in perfect harmony. All this was his, plus acres of orange, lemon and cashew-nut groves. Dennis arranged for us to have a three-day break at the Kruger National Park, staying in thatched huts at one of the sites, and getting up at dawn as the best time to catch sight of animals. On the first day we were fortunate to witness a cheetah stalking and catching his prey. We watched a huge African elephant walk along the road in front of our car, with others by the side of the road. I loved the very special atmosphere of the park, which I hadn't visited since I was a child, and appreciated being in the hands of an experienced old friend with all his acquired knowledge of the region. He had booked two thatched huts for our accommodation, but we used only one of them, the other being useful as a separate kitchen where we stored our food. On arriving back at the estate, we learned that Margaret was returning earlier than expected! Soon after

I was put on a plane back to Johannesburg, with my ticket paid for. Had word been sent to her by neighbours we met at the park that I was a threat? I never found out. Before leaving for London I had an opportunity of visiting the Sterkfontein caves, famous for their early archaeological finds.

In October I had an interview to join the Association of Humanistic Practitioners, and the following year I facilitated a workshop on the theme of *synthesis* for the association. This particular weekend sticks in my mind for the pain I was in from a slipped disc. I followed that year with another workshop at the association's conference at the University of Surrey, with the theme *transforming crisis*, where on arrival I was greeted by the president (who had known me when we were both involved with a television programme at the BBC). He was so carried away with enthusiasm that he lifted and swung me off my feet, resulting in the fracture of one or more ribs! Once more I found myself running a workshop in considerable pain.

During that year I was back in Amsterdam sleeping on the floor of the Cosmos while attending a retreat on the subject of peace with Thich Nhat Hanh, the Vietnamese meditation teacher. I was also fortunate enough to witness the slight, bent, smiling figure of the Dalai Lama inspiring an audience of 6,000 of us at the Royal Albert Hall with his talk "Peace of Mind, Peace in Action".

That summer I joined a group of Namgyal Rinpoche's

European students on an ancient barge on the Seine, where we created our own classes each day, taking it in turns to offer work. It was good to spend time with some of the European dharma students. I was back in England in time to run a holiday course with two friends presenting yoga, painting and photography at Micklepage, a charming small centre in Sussex. From there I went straight on to a GRTA conference to run a dance workshop!

In October we had our final examinations, as conclusion of the three-year clinical psychotherapy course, held at Guy's Hospital. The following morning I drove down to Somerset to run another of my weekend workshops, this one entitled Turning Point. I loved giving these workshops. Enabling participants to delve deeply into themselves and discover how they could change their lives was enormously satisfying. My spiritual background, through my practice of yoga and Buddhist meditation, gave me the emotional strength and physical stamina to support these brave people.

I had now decided to leave London again and find a house in the Glastonbury area, where I had begun to be known, and could be assured of future work. Before doing so I made another trip to South Africa for my parents' sixtieth wedding anniversary. My brother joined us from his home in Israel and we set about searching for a suitable retirement home for them, while he stayed on to make the necessary arrangements. On returning to

London I was met with the news that a great friend, Don, had died some days earlier at the age of forty. The news was not unexpected, as he was very ill with melanoma before I left, but I wished I could have been back for the funeral, the day before. Instead I was able to accompany his widow, Lesley, to collect his ashes. I had tried to advise Don to change his diet, and had been treating him with reflexology, but it was too late. The cancer was already too far advanced. When I last saw him, in a bed made up for him in his living room, I had taken a loving farewell of him.

Move to Somerset

In December I left my flat in Putney where I had lived for twenty-one years, apart from the two years at my cottage in the Forest of Dean. I arranged to share a house in Redhill, near Bristol, with a couple of dharma friends for a few months while I looked for a house in Somerset. After Melanie and her partner Paul had joined us for Christmas, I left for a conference on peace at Findhorn and on my return commenced house-hunting in earnest, while starting a weekly therapy group at the Butleigh centre. I revisited a lovely detached cottage in West Pennard, which I had seen before going to South Africa, and loved, but thought the price was too high. The owners had recently reduced it as they were desperate to sell. The wife was suffering from depression and wanted to leave the area. Two months later I moved in. Some weeks after I learned that the woman had taken her life. Moving house hadn't been the answer!

While running my annual yoga course at Hawkwood College that Easter, I answered a phone call from my brother in South Africa informing me that my father had died. Following the weekend course I was due at a five-day conference at Dartington Hall on the meaning of illness, where I was to run a daily workshop. I could see no way of dropping everything and getting to the funeral in Johannesburg. On top of those commitments I was finalising the purchase of Willow Cottage in West Pennard. There was no time for mourning during this intense period. That would have to wait till later. The day after I finally moved into my new house I ran a weekend workshop at Lower Rocks in Butleigh, now almost on my doorstep, called New Beginnings!

In May I was delighted to attend the opening ceremony of the Japanese Buddhist stupa in Battersea Park. This religious monument had been built by a Buddhist order of Japanese monks dedicated to erecting these peace stupas in a number of countries around the world. As part of a group of invited guests, I was treated to a packed lunch of Japanese food in the rain, after a moving ceremony. Back in Somerset I prepared to co-facilitate a two-year training course for the Institute for the Development of Human Potential at Openings, a therapy centre in Bath, where I was also to have a practice seeing clients, for the next three years. For my own learning, I embarked on monthly weekend trainings in biosynthesis with David Boadella, also at Openings, while beginning to see private clients at my lovely new home near Glastonbury.

That summer of 1985 I flew to Zürich for a ten-day meditation Kālachakra retreat with the Dalai Lama at

Rikon, a town with the largest community of Tibetans living in Europe. My accommodation was in a dormitory in an underground nuclear bunker. This proved to be a wonderfully rich experience, with teachings in a vast marquee with several hundred Tibetans and fellow-Europeans. There was also time off to picnic and bathe in the nearby river. On the 1st August we celebrated the Dalai Lama's fiftieth birthday, after which I walked up the hill through grassy fields to the Tibetan monastery where he resided. I had never felt happier!

The following year of 1986 turned out to be a particularly difficult one. After setting up an eight-week therapy group in Bristol with the male therapist who would be my co-facilitator on the two-year IDHP training course, called Facilitator Styles, we braved the group of students, among whom were some who had been rejected the year before. Whether this was the reason for their highly confrontational stance, I do not know. What I do know is that I was not used to working with such students, and found it very difficult, being reduced to tears on more than one occasion. I was learning how cruel a group could be to a mother figure! In the Easter holidays I took a flight to Denmark to visit Melanie who had been teaching at the Theatre Academy in Århus for nine months. It was there that I had the experience of viewing frozen waves from the seashore – a wonderful sight!

About this time my brother Theo and his wife arrived

in England from their home in Haifa, bringing with them my mother, now in her eighties, who was living with them. Since they were in need of a break from her, they urged me to take up my filial duties and have her to stay for six weeks. It couldn't have been at a worse time! I drove up to London to fetch her. She had become quite helpless since my father's death, and the fear that had always been there in her personality had now become palpable. For the first time in my life she alluded to the secret in her background that she said had affected her whole life. "It has also affected mine," I told her. This was the story that I had learned only as a teenager, by reading letters I found hidden away in my mother's wardrobe in Johannesburg, relating the family tragedy. They were letters from my mother's uncle in Sunderland to my father, prior to their marriage. They told of how her father had left England in order to go ahead and make a new life for his family in South Africa shortly before the First World War. His wife and six children were therefore prevented from following him. In what turned out to be only a couple of months before the end of the war, his wife foolishly deciding to risk the journey to join him, setting out from Southampton on a troop ship, the *Galway Castle*. Two days out at sea the ship was torpedoed, with passengers flung into the freezing water. Women and young children were assigned to the lifeboats, but the one my mother, her mother and siblings were in, overturned. None of them could swim.

Somehow my mother and her brother Jack were miraculously saved. Out of a family of seven, only my mother, aged thirteen, and her brother aged sixteen, survived by clinging onto pieces of debris, until rescued many hours later, and taken back to England. Apparently neither knew if any of the rest of their family was alive. They were taken to separate hospitals, and later sent back to their home in Sunderland, to be cared for by an uncle and aunt. It is difficult to imagine how a girl of that age, coming from a protected background, could cope with such a disaster, and she subsequently learned to protect herself with a curtain of secrecy and denial. At a later date the two children were finally sent out to South Africa again to join their father. I am so thankful for her survival, as it led to my and Melanie's existence. We have both been deeply affected by this story. My grandfather lived with us through my childhood, as did her brother Jack, until he married, and I was aware then of how much resentment and anger she continued to feel towards her father, without my understanding why. Such a secret, locked away in the family archives, was reflected in my mother's behaviour while I was growing up. All cupboards in the house would be kept locked. Her explanation for this was that it was to prevent the servants stealing our goods and food. The effect on me was to feel locked out, of not being trusted, of not belonging, a sense that has remained with me all my life – that of being a black sheep in the community, and always the outsider looking in. I am also reminded of a holiday we had when I was about nine years old. On crossing a stream with a friend, with my parents, and with a friend of theirs called Harry, my mother refused to move until Harry picked her up and carried her across. Unfortunately he dropped her in the water, and my mother, in an extremely distressed state, was led away. I didn't see her for the next couple of days. My friend and I, left to our own devices, decided to visit a nearby native village of mud huts. We watched naked black children playing in the dust, while women prepared and cooked the communal meal on an open fire. Not surprisingly I felt particularly drawn to black women as they had cared for me as a young child. I retained a strong impression of the pungent smell and warmth of their bodies.

Trying to attend to my mother's needs, while seeing clients at home and in Bath, and continuing to run the IDHP course there, proved particularly stressful. I arranged for her to attend a day centre on days when I was away, and a friend came down from Essex to help me out when I co-facilitated a five-day residential course in Cornwall. We had a visit from my brother and his wife shortly before I took her back to London and saw her off at Gatwick, to my great relief!

The following week I joined a ten-day summer dance camp, where I taught a daily yoga class. On the evening of the eighth day I joined a late-night contact dance session in a marquee. I was so enjoying close contact with a young man that I leaped exuberantly into the air, my feet slipped on the damp grass floor, and I ended up in the splits, tearing a ligament in my right leg. I was carried to someone's caravan and spent the night in considerable pain. Melanie, who was staying at Willow Cottage at the time, was sent for to take me home. The Rinpoche was due to arrive the next day to give a four-day course at my home, while I was unable to stand, let alone walk! I was therefore forced to hand over all responsibility to others – a good lesson for me. Unable to sit cross-legged on the floor as I was used to doing, I listened to the teachings stretched out on a couch.

A week later I joined some Crystal Group members to travel to Scotland. There we hired a splendid Brixham trawler to explore the Outer Hebrides. We crewed this beautiful wooden panelled sailing craft, which came with its own skipper and cook, while visiting Iona and Fingal's Cave, and anchoring overnight at Tiree and Colonsay. In spite of being handicapped by my weak leg, which made it difficult getting in and out of the boat, I enjoyed the trip enormously, particularly the quality of light in that area.

At the beginning of 1987 I went into therapy with Paul Zeal from the Richmond Fellowship in London, who had settled in Taunton. He used the Freudian model I was interested in exploring. In particular I was keen to work on my inability to form an intimate relationship. I was aware that having lost two young husbands in tragic circumstances there was a fear of a repeat situation if I ever allowed myself to become emotionally involved with another man.

In May I joined a workshop on death on the Greek island of Hydra, run by a friend of mine, Margot Grey, with whom I had stayed in Shoreham while she wrote her book *Return from Death*, about near-death experience. Even as a small child I was always fascinated by the subject of where we go to when we die, and I continue to believe firmly in reincarnation. A small group of us took part in morning classes and seminars in the home of friends of Margot's, while the afternoons were spent in exploring this vehicle-less island. The second week was spent visiting Epídavros on the mainland, picnicking at a Roman site, swimming in a very cold sea, watching splendid sunsets, and indulging in long evenings at the taverna. A doctor friend of Margot's was writing a book on past-life experiences, and invited me to allow myself to be hypnotised by him at his home in Guildford. Back in England, soon after the commencement of the session, I began to cough and choke, and reported being surrounded by smoke while tied to a pole. I felt I was being burned at the stake. That life proceeded to unfold backwards. I talked of living in a rural part of Scotland as a wise woman working with the making of herbal concoctions, sometime in the seventeenth century. Earlier I had been part of a group of warring men, as a young woman, servicing them and generally looking after their needs, and as a child I had lived with my grandmother in a primitive hovel in the woods. A few weeks later I had a follow-up session, where I learned that the judge who sentenced me to death as a witch, was my present-day mother, which may account for the difficult relationship I had with her, and my experiencing her as harmful to me. It felt good to end the session by forgiving her. That same day I had arranged to visit a couple who had been members of the primal integration group with Bill Swartley in the 1970s. They reminded me that at that time the group had re-experienced a past-life episode in which they appeared to be a seventeenth-century Scottish clan of dangerous marauding men. I had been unable to identify with them, yet I felt part of the scene. Did the early part of my past life, as revealed under hypnosis, explain why, and did that account for my preoccupation with the character of Joan of Arc and her burning at the stake?

At the end of May I went down to Devon to join a meeting of therapists, psychiatrists and healers intent on procuring a beautiful house, chapel and outbuildings in a valley that contained the Hazelwood Estate, set in terraced gardens and fields leading down to a river below. The idea was to raise £2,000,000 within six weeks to run this charming house as a therapeutic/healing centre. I still held the dream of living and working in such an environment. Unfortunately we were unable to raise the necessary amount in such a short space of time and the scheme had to be abandoned.

In July I was fortunate to attend one of the most exciting theatrical events of my life, given by a Russian company at the Riverside Theatre in London, entitled *Cerceau*. The audience sat three sides round a central set of a wooden dacha. All the action took place over a weekend in the open-walled home and garden of a group of family and friends, during a summer-house party. The audience were encouraged to change their seating area during the performance to gain an alternative view into the rooms during each scene. This was a beautifully acted, uniquely exciting production that I will never forget!

That summer I flew to Majorca to visit Amanda, whom I had known since she was a baby. Her grandmother was Freda, an old theatre friend from South Africa. Amanda was working as a nanny with a family living near Valldemossa. After spending a few days at a hotel by the sea at Port de Sóller, I returned to Palma to meet up with a new friend. My therapy had borne fruit, and I was having a delightful relationship with this Welshman living at the foot of Glastonbury Tor! We flew to Ibiza for a few hedonistic days of beautiful meals and champagne, sleeping under the stars on a mattress spread out on the flat roof of his apartment. On returning to Mallorca I went to find Ingrid, an old German friend, living in a casita with an orchard of almonds and figs she had bought a few years earlier.

Back in England I continued to see therapy clients, run

a weekly therapy group at the house, teach yoga at Strode College, and attend a dance class, while the Crystal Group were now using my lovely meditation room one weekend a month. In October I joined a two-year course in Bristol entitled East West Psychotherapy and Spirituality, consisting of monthly seminars, which came to grief after nine months!

At the beginning of 1988 I took to my bed with tonsillitis, which became serious when it developed into quinsy, where the infection in my throat was affecting my breathing and spreading up the side of my face to my ear. With the infection threatening to move up to my brain, I was forced to accept antibiotics for the first time in my life. I had long been averse to antibiotics, knowing that they knock out the immune system. Having been brought up as a Christian Scientist I had never taken medical drugs, preferring to rely on alternative methods. After ten days in bed, and beginning to improve, I began a course of acupuncture.

Soon after going back to work I began to run a weekend training in Gestalt and bodywork at the Centre for Counselling and Psychotherapy Education at their building in Notting Hill Gate. About this time I also put Willow Cottage on the market. Melanie and her partner Paul had been renting a house in Bristol, which had become too expensive for them to return to after touring with their theatre company Intimate Strangers, in Europe and Britain, during the last few years. My big cottage in

West Pennard had not developed into the healing/therapeutic centre I had originally envisaged. I had been too busy with clients and courses. Melanie approached me with the proposition to sell the house and offer them enough capital from the proceeds to buy a house for them in that area, and a smaller home for me. It made such good sense that I gave an immediate positive response. It left me free to choose where to move. Two destinations came to mind – Totnes and Italy. Totnes in Devon is where Melanie had been a student at Dartington College of Arts, and where she was now a freelance tutor in the theatre department. In spite of a warning that there were already too many therapists working there, I opted for Totnes. I think I welcomed the idea of less work. I was beginning to suffer from burnout. I put an advert in the local Totnes newspaper for a house to buy, and received one reply. I viewed it and agreed to buy it in spite of the fact that it had not been valued. It seemed quite suitable – particularly also for a friend of Melanie's who needed a home in Totnes while she studied at the college.

With enough money available from the sale of the cottage, I decided to do a world trip. There was so much of the world I wanted to see and so many cultures to experience, and now was a good time to go before starting up a new practice, and before getting any older. A month after moving to Totnes, I had the good fortune to do a ten-day retreat in France with Ram Dass, the well-known guru of the '60s, camping in the grounds of a chateau. There was a hair-raising drive down to the centre of the country with two friends from Glastonbury, with none of us ever having driven on the right before, but it was worth it to be with Ram Dass, who I was about to meet in California again very soon.

Round the World Trip, USA

After buying a round-the-world ticket for £922, I set off in September for New York on the first lap of my six-month journey. After three days with Nina (an actress I had treated with reflexology in London) at her home in Douglaston, outside New York, I took a train to Boston to stay with Marcia, who now lived in Cambridge, working at Harvard University. It was lovely seeing her again, and meeting her daughter and dog. We had last met when I visited her in Halifax, Nova Scotia, with Melanie, in 1974. Four days later I was off to San Francisco to stay an uncomfortable couple of days with a friend's sister in Oakland, whose marriage was falling apart, then by bus to Santa Rosa and the Rancho Tropicano for an international transpersonal conference spanning seven days of intense lectures and workshops with the likes of Ram Dass, Stanislav Grof, Jack Cornfield, Charles Tart, Arnold Mindell, Sogyal Rinpoche, Joanna Macey, Marilyn Ferguson, Tai Chi master Chungliang Al Huang and Dulce and Michael Murphy of the Esalen Institute. The purely academic sessions left me cold. How can anyone present in any depth, and answer questions in the forty-five minutes allotted to the speakers? What I enjoyed most were the meditations, the movement sessions and the musical interludes. I was deeply moved by Dulce Murphy (wife of Michael, co-founder of Esalen), talking on the subject of her nine-year involvement at Esalen in Soviet-American relations. I talked with her later and expressed the desire to see something on the same lines taking place in Britain. I was moved by Al Huang's energy and sheer joy in movement, and loved dancing with him; by Paul Horn's flute playing, particularly in the accompanying film of his communication with an orca killer whale that had lost its long-term mate; by Jack Cornfield's gentle meditational approach; and by Ram Dass's and Joannna Macey's passion. Another moving experience was Rusty Schweickart, the astronaut, having come straight from a gathering of colleagues in Budapest, showing slides from photographs of Earth from space, with statements from other astronauts and cosmonauts.

At the end of the conference I indulged myself with a stay at Harbin Hot Springs, where a couple I knew from Glastonbury were living. One could stroll from one pool to another with varying temperatures ranging from quite hot to boiling, in which to soak without a stitch on, and feel quite comfortable doing so. After three days of such hedonism, planning to go on to Seattle, I posted a note on a notice board requesting a lift from anyone going north in the next few days, and received a reply from a young man named Bill due to return to work on one of the St Juan islands, where he lived.

We set off the next day in his old Ford van through the magnificent redwood forests. Stopping at Eureka for the night we shared a room. The next night was spent at a lakeside site, when I slept in the van. On the third day we drove along the beautiful Oregon coast. Stopping at Honeyman Park, Bill gathered chanterelle mushrooms and cooked them over an open fire with some onions for a succulent meal. That day I meditated in a cave, watched a sunset at Foul Weather Point (named by Captain Cook who landed there in a storm), and camped for the night at Tillamook Bay. The following day we finally crossed the Columbia River into Washington State and Seattle where I had arranged to stay with Pat, mother of another Glastonbury friend. I hadn't wanted that journey to end. I felt so happy and carefree, like a character in Jack Kerouac's novel *On the Road*. Bill turned out to be a perfect companion, relaxed and easy to be with. He had actually taken off several extra days from work on my account instead of going straight back home, for which I was very grateful. The magical time continued with a ferry ride a few days later to stay overnight at Bainbridge Island with a therapist I had met at Santa Rosa. After a drive round the island and a visit to a Buddhist community, we had dinner and soaked in a hot tub under a full moon at her house, high up overlooking the twinkling lights of Seattle across the water. This was one place where I felt I could come back to live. The following day, after returning to the city, I travelled with friend April and her mother by boat to Orcas Island, one of the St Juan islands, where Pat would be running a three-day yoga course at the Theosophical Society Centre there. This is the island where Richard Bach lived, author of *Jonathan Livingston Seagull.* I offered a yoga and creative dance class while there, and spent a lovely few days enjoying the scenery, and rabbits, which were everywhere! A few days later I was able to get a ferry from Orcas to Vancouver Island. I had arranged to stay with Marcia's ex-partner Doug and their son Damian. Doug had also stayed with me at Ravenna Road in Putney in the 1970s. I arrived in time for Halloween and was asked to judge the costumes at a Halloween party the next night. Journeying on to Vancouver, I stayed with Sue and Bill, who had run the centre, White Rocks, where I had given yoga classes while living at the cottage in the Forest of Dean. The memory I am left with about that time in Vancouver was the constant rain. During the seven days I was there it barely ever stopped! I was told what a beautiful city it is in the summer! Early one morning I took a bus back to Seattle and a final visit to Bainbridge Island.

Heading south with Colin, another Glastonbury friend, on his way to San Francisco, I asked him to drop me off at Yreka in order to experience a spiritual teacher I was curious to meet. She was called Pearl, giving teachings on the ascended masters, near Mount Shasta, a sacred mountain. Arriving at Yreka at three a.m., a one-horse town in the middle of nowhere, I booked into a motel for the rest of the night. After a day spent trying to make contact with Pearl, to my surprise a beautiful white convertible arrived to collect me, with Kirk, a young man, also in white, at the wheel. The next day I moved into a room in the small town of Mount Shasta, attending meetings led by Pearl, in which she purported to channel the ascended masters, while the weather grew colder and turned to snow. Although I found her channelling rather strange, including messages from the master Jesus, I continued to remain open to other ideas and beliefs. On the last of my five days there, I was taken up the sacred mountain with a spade to dig a hole in the earth beneath the snow in order to plant some sacred items I had brought with me from Ireland and Scotland, and at the same time collect some earth, in the now empty containers, to take back to Glastonbury to bury on the Tor there, it being another sacred mount.

Arriving back in San Francisco, after being laid up with a bout of 'flu, I began to attend yoga classes, and was glad to discover Berkeley University and the Nyngma Institute, a Tibetan monastery, within walking distance of where I was staying. One day I took a bus to Mill Valley to visit Jack Painter who had taught the Reichian massage and breath work at the Churchill Centre that I used with clients and in my workshops, and which I would continue to teach for years to come. Another time I joined Jalaja, a therapist friend for a weekend workshop of Gestalt therapy at a beautiful coastal retreat.

Finally, after three weeks, with a final day of Buddhist meditation with Dudjom Dorjee, I took a bus to Monterey on my way to Esalen, the growth centre at Big Sur, where I was due to spend a month as a work student. I had decided to go as a work student as I wanted to experience Esalen as a member of the community rather than as a visitor. On arrival I found I was to share a room with three others at South Coast, a mile along the road to the centre. One of my roommates turned out to be a farmer from north Devon who kept me awake at night with his snoring! I enjoyed the early morning walk along the main coastal road each morning to start work in the kitchen by seven o'clock, and often got a lift back in the evening, which I needed after cooking for up to 200 people four days a week on five-hour shifts. However I managed to find time to take part in psychodrama and Gestalt groups, attend choir and dance practice, have the odd massage, and best of all soak in the hot pools overlooking the sea. On more than one occasion there was the rare sight of orca or killer whales spouting close to the shore on their way south for the winter – an unforgettable sight! To my great surprise and pleasure I discovered Bill Swartley's three children and a grandchild living in the community, when his widow, Bea, living nearby at Carmel, came to visit. I had met their youngest daughter when Bill was living in my flat in London. Meeting them unleashed an emotional floodgate, and I found myself having to deal with former unresolved feelings of loss and abandonment. Bill had been an important part of my life. Bea came up to congratulate me after I read the channelled words of Jesus to a huge gathering on Christmas Day. I had been asked to give a reading, and I guessed this might be suitable material for the day! It apparently went down very well as people continued to congratulate me over the next few days.

On 9th January I left this former sacred Indian site after a wonderful month, though professionally I wished I had been there at least a dozen years earlier, when I would have benefited from the therapy experience, whereas I felt that my own therapy work had developed and become more subtle while some of the humanistic techniques I found there were stuck in the past. Hugo, the Devon farmer, offered to drive me to Los Angeles, where I had arranged to stay with Simon, a former boyfriend of Melanie's. On the way we stopped to visit Hurst Castle at St Simeon, the famous newspaper magnate's former mansion. At Santa Barbara we visited the Ojai Foundation, set up by Joan Halifax, the Buddhist teacher and writer, formerly married to Stanislav Grof. Set in lovely gardens, I hoped to spend more time there one day. After a nightmare experience of trying to find the exit off the freeway in Los Angeles, I was finally safely delivered to Simon's house.

My sixtieth birthday on 20th January proved to be an unexpected day! I had arranged to meet the parents of a friend at the University of Los Angeles where they worked. I had a forty-five minute wait for a bus, and arrived late, just as they had given up on me and were leaving for home. There was time only for a few words of apology and the receiving of a birthday present they had brought for me, and I was back on a returning bus. It was getting dark by the time I arrived downtown where I needed to find another bus back to where I was staying. While I looked for a bus stop I was approached by an Indian girl who warned me against being on the street alone. It was unusual for her to be out on her own in the dark, she told me. Her family usually came to meet her from work. She advised me to ring for a taxi, but too dangerous from a phone booth nearby. The best thing was for me to come home with her and ring from there. On reaching her house I was warmly greeted by her family and invited to stay for tea. When I mentioned it was my birthday, her mother disappeared into the kitchen reappearing soon after with a large fruitcake. Finally the family decided to drive me home. We left in a convoy of two cars, and they waited until they saw me safely indoors. I was deeply touched by their concern for a perfect stranger, and hoped I could reciprocate somehow in the future.

Hawaii

The next day I flew to Honolulu. A young woman I met at Esalen, who had been living there, asked if she could accompany me on my travels, as she was nervous of travelling alone. She subsequently booked on my flights to Hawaii, Japan and Singapore. I had arranged to do a yoga course on the Big Island at a lovely centre, Kalani Hanua, meaning *harmony of heaven and earth*, in the jungle. During the course the participants were taken on exciting expeditions, caving, surfing and visiting the local volcano. We walked across a lava path there, and only the next day we learned the volcano had erupted during the night, hurling tons of rock into the sea. What timing! At the end of the course I flew to Maui with Bridget, where we hired a car and made our way to a YMCA, sleeping in primitive bunk beds, plagued by mosquitoes. We spent the next two days exploring the area, but what with endless rain, and a growing tension developing between us, I began to feel quite depressed. I felt that Bridget had unresolved mother issues and I was taking the flak! The situation came to a head when we were driving with our luggage to the other side of the island, and I mentioned a dream I had had the night before featuring a fatal crash, and suggested that she didn't need to drive quite so fast as we were not in a hurry to get anywhere. At that she exploded and ordered me out of the car. We were passing near the airport and I persuaded her to let me out there. I managed to get a flight to Honolulu, and booked into a hotel on the beach. Meanwhile I really enjoyed the next few days being escorted round the island, taken snorkelling, and out to dinner by an eager young man I met, before spending a few days with Caroline, whom I had met at the Santa Rosa conference, in her apartment overlooking a beautiful Japanese garden.

Japan

The next stop was Tokyo. Sitting behind me on the plane was Bridget, and I managed to squeeze out a few friendly words. We arrived at Narita Airport after a nine-hour journey. I was due to stay with Karl, another of Melanie's ex-boyfriends. I was to ring him from the airport, whereupon he would direct me to where he lived in Kamakura. On dialling his number I was met with a message that he had gone to Thailand, and wouldn't be back for a week. There was a personal message for me giving me directions – Japanese names delivered in a German accent, of how to reach his house, which I was totally unable to decipher. Before collapsing in despair I remembered I had the phone number of a student of Rinpoche's who had married a Japanese woman and was now living in Tokyo. I sent up a prayer that he would be there to answer the phone, and to my considerable relief he was, and miraculously offered to meet me at a hotel that I could reach by bus from the airport. On our meeting I discovered that Peter and his wife Eiko had taken a bus, a train and a taxi to reach me! I was so grateful to them for offering me a bed for three nights, showing me round the city, and finally putting me on the bullet train for Kyoto. On arrival at the station I spent at least half an hour trying to find the exit, as naturally all the signs were in Japanese. At the nearby information office I was given the name of a traditional inn, and found it only with the help of an old woman I passed on my way, who directed me after reading the address on the slip of paper I clutched in my hand, together with my luggage. My experience of the language and the environment felt so alien that once in my room I didn't dare venture out for the rest of that day.

The next morning I rang the number of a friend's former ikebana teacher, and as it was a public holiday he offered to collect me and take me out for the day. Nakano Sensei arrived with his beautiful wife and equally beautiful student to take me first to breakfast and then on to visit Buddhist and Shinto temples, an exhibition of traditional crafts and an exhibit of ikebana, all of high quality. By the evening we met up with several of his students for dinner. Mary, an American woman, invited me to visit her the next day. I bravely took a subway train to her station. Unable to read the names of the stations I managed by counting the number we passed. I was entranced by her ancient traditional house, which appeared to be made of parchment walls and sloping wooden floors.

After two enjoyable days I checked out of my Japanese inn and went to stay with another contact, a Japanese

English teacher in Osaka, surprisingly living in a Western-style house with Western furniture. It wasn't until the following day that I met her husband, who as a typical Japanese businessman went straight from work to social recreation each evening. Meanwhile I had heard from Karl that he had finally arrived home. I was welcome to come and stay and he would meet me at the station in Tokyo. Sure enough he was there on the platform holding a single red rose – "A rose for Ros" was his greeting. With him was Eliza, an American girlfriend he had met on his visit to Thailand, and was so smitten that he had to return to wait for her while she finished her meditation retreat on the island of Kho Pha Ngan. This was the reason he wasn't at home for my visit. In spite of the fact that they were obviously very much in love, and it must have been a pain for them to have me around, they made me feel welcome, and made an effort to make my stay enjoyable. I was able to spend time at the great Green Buddha at Engaku-ji Temple in Kamakura, while I had the exciting experience of being taken to Okahama to join Karl's dance class on two occasions with the famous dance master, Ono, founder of Butoh Theatre, who referred to me as "England" during the class. Another exciting experience was a performance at the Kabuki Theatre in Tokyo, which lasted from 4.30 to 9 p.m.!

Malaysia and Thailand

Now I was on my way to Thailand via Singapore, where I had to collect a visa. Once again I found Bridget on my plane! During a three-day wait for my visa, I posted home clothes I didn't need, and booked a railway ticket for Penang. Finally, armed with a visa for Thailand, I travelled overnight to Kuala Lumpur and then on to Penang. I spent three days in a cheap lodging in the Chinese quarter, where I was warned to double padlock my bedroom door for safety, and felt very nervous with the sound of men going past all night to a filthy rat-infested toilet in the yard. Meanwhile I learned of a minibus travelling to Surat Thani in the south of Thailand, from where I could reach Wat Suan Mokkh, the meditation retreat centre where I had planned to do a ten-day retreat. On arrival at Suan Mokkh I settled into the daily routine of rising at four in the morning, attending a talk by the well-known teacher Adjha Buddhassa at 4.45, after which there was a half-hour sitting in meditation, an hour of yoga practise, and another talk before breakfast at eight o'clock. The rest of the day was spent in walking and sitting meditation, interspersed with meals before bedtime at 9.30. The weather was very hot. I had been feeling homesick for some time, and I found myself doing a lot of planning about what I would do on my return home. The women's quarters were in a long building with thin mattresses on the floor, and we were warned to watch out for snakes. One evening my torch gave out on my way to my sleeping quarters, and I remained standing petrified in the dark until discovered by another working torch. I was unable to call out as the retreat was in silence. However I was invited to teach the yoga class each morning where, as the instructor, I was able to speak for that hour each day. At the end of the retreat the participants spent a day splashing about in a nearby watering hole, which was an enormous treat. After a train to Surat Thani, I spent several idyllic days swimming in the waters round the islands of Ko Samui and Ko Pha Ngan, then on to Bangkok for two days at the Truly Yours Guest House. Leaving the heat, dust and noise of the city I gladly travelled north to visit Venetia, a friend from Totnes, who still lives there with her partner, Inson. Venetia is a dedicated Theravadan Buddhist, and has since created a magnificent dharma park at her home, with significant sculpture works she has created. During the five days I spent with Venetia I made several visits to nearby Chang Mai, being shown around the city by Marvin, a young American, while riding on the back of his motorcycle. He also took me to the airport to catch a plane for Bangkok and the journey home, on this the final phase of my six-month journey round the world.

Sometime after my arrival home I wrote about my experience as a journey of exploration. What I learned from it was the lesson of breaking my habitual mould of work and giving myself more time and space. I learned to live more consciously in the present, and to trust my invisible guides (I had felt protected at all times). I believe I developed a wider perspective, and clearer understanding of my life and work, while travelling through other countries gave me a greater appreciation of my own country, and in particular of Devon, the county in which I live. Most important of all I discovered that everything I seek is right here within me!

Totnes

B ack in Totnes, where I had left the friend renting my house, I encountered her dissatisfaction with having to share it with me, and so she moved out, while I went ahead with having the loft converted to a bedroom for myself. I started to do some individual and group work at the Natural Health Centre, and after a while began to take on private clients for psychotherapy at home. I continued to give my Easter weekend workshops at Hawkwood College, and ran another of my annual weekend training workshops of Gestalt and bodywork at the Centre for Counselling and Psychotherapy Education in London. I continued to run these trainings for the next ten years. The most significant event of that year for me was gaining a lover – a tall spare Irishman, with whom I spent the spring and summer exploring Dartmoor and enjoying long lazy days on Slapton Beach nearby. There were friends from Holland, London and Glastonbury to stay, and I was happy to have a boyfriend – though not for long. Within the year he disappeared to Japan and then on to Australia!

Ruins at Pisac, Peru, 1982

Expedition into the rain forest down the Rio
Madre de Dios, Peru, 1982

Great Buddha at Kamakura, Japan, 1989

Temple at Changmai, Thailand, 1989

Moving on the beach at Hawaii Big Island, 1988

Willow Cottage, West Pennard, Somerset, 1985

PART FIVE
1990–1999

The Workshop Facilitator and Trainer

Achievement

Personal Growth
and Training Workshops

This was the year of Nelson Mandela's release into the outside world after twenty-six years of imprisonment. I was in London for a Crystal Group meeting, and on 11th February I made for Trafalgar Square to await the momentous event, and to join in the celebrations. Needless to say, I was deeply moved. It seemed to me that this was the moment I had been waiting for all my adult life. When the moment was announced I joined thousands of others in an exuberant dance of joy in the square. What an emotional outpouring that was! Growing up in South Africa, unlike most of the white population, I seemed to have a natural empathy with the country's native black people. At that time we referred to them as natives. I enjoyed the way they sang while doing heavy manual work, and in my mother's kitchen in the evenings, the servants would harmonise together. There was Andrew, our garden "boy", and a succession of constantly changing house "girls", who were all natural singers. When I was older there were occasions when I was banished from the table for some unknown demeanour, and was expected to finish my meal in the kitchen, which was never a hardship. I actually preferred the company of the servants. Although I left the country shortly before the official introduction of Apartheid, I was sufficiently disturbed by the inequality of white and black, and the degrading position held by the latter, which I witnessed daily, that I was happy to escape the country as soon as I had earned enough money to pay for my ticket to England. I sensed that if I stayed I would sooner or later land in prison for my beliefs.

At this time I was offering more weekend training workshops in bodywork psychotherapy and Gestalt at the Centre for Counselling and Psychotherapy Education in London, and seeing clients privately from the college. In Totnes I began a weekly bodywork group at the Totnes Natural Health Centre. I taught a form of Reichian breathing I had used for many years with clients. This practice could produce an altered state of consciousness, which would gain access to deep early memories, including sometimes what appeared to be past-life experiences. I found this an effective tool for resolving and finally healing painful and disturbingly persistent life problems.

That summer I travelled to Israel for my niece Judith's wedding in Jerusalem. Here I was able to see my mother again. There was an opportunity to visit her in an old people's home and begin to connect on a more personal level. I encouraged her to talk about her first meeting with my father and their subsequent marriage. This was the first occasion that she had talked about herself in this way, and it felt like an important breakthrough!

In 1991 I devised a weekend residential course to run at Dartington Hall, which continued annually for the next seven years. I was delighted to have the chance to combine my skills in yoga, dance, massage, visualisation and meditation etc. in creating a course entitled Nurturing Ourselves, and to offer a relaxing, healing experience. Melanie was still teaching at the college of arts there and continued to do so until its demise many years later.

In June I took an overnight train from Swansea to Cork for a meditation course with the Rinpoche at the cottage the Crystal Group had bought the year before in southern Ireland near Kenmare, on the teacher's instruction, to use as a centre. I had to leave after a week in order to get to London to obtain a visa for Russia, where I was planning to go in July. When I left, the teacher waved me off, and I took the gesture seriously as a dismissal. I had been sitting too long a time at the teacher's feet, and it was time for me to go. It was to be four years before I would meet him again!

Russia

I had been accepted by the Association of Humanistic Psychology to represent Britain with three or four others, at the association's first international conference in Moscow. After the meeting in Santa Rosa with delegates involved in dialogue with colleagues in Russia, I felt inspired to have such an opportunity myself. On arrival at Moscow Airport, the British delegation for the conference was met by the American Saybrook University bus carrying their large delegation, and we were driven some thirty kilometres to an adult education centre in Galicino, a country area. On the first day the foreign visitors were taken to Moscow for a tour of the Kremlin, where I came upon Raisa Gorbachev, wife of the president, chatting with a small group of people. Tragically she was to die of cancer not long after. There was another couple of visits to Moscow during the conference's sometimes unendurably long lectures in the Soviet style. I was fascinated to visit the cemetery where Chekhov, Khrushchev and many other famous Russian figures were buried.

I and a drama therapist from Bristol, Tone, made up

our minds to present a workshop each to demonstrate an alternative approach to the conference. On offering my bodywork psychotherapy workshop, to my astonishment I found forty Russians and one American eager to participate. We were allocated a most inappropriate space – a kind of lobby at the top of some stairs where I was forced to improvise, having the students lying on bare carpet without cushions to do the exercises. When it came to using movement, where I was accustomed to the use of taped music, which I didn't have with me, fortunately there was someone to play a piano that just happened to be in the space! The workshop proved to be a great success, and afterwards I was approached by Vladimir, the director of a bodywork institute in Moscow, and also by the head of the psychology department at Moscow University, inviting me to return and run workshops for them that same year.

I had planned to take a train to Leningrad, as it was still called at that time, but as I had developed a chest infection and a temperature, arrangements were made by the conference organisers for me to stay on in Moscow with a medical couple, Vera and Victor, in their flat on the outskirts of the city. Fortunately I was treated during the next few days by Jacob Markov, a doctor I had met at the conference. He used an accepted folk medicine method of curing my cough by applying a mixture of vodka and ginger on my chest and the soles of my feet! I discovered that Jacob was a yoga teacher, who had been forced to teach secretly in a hidden basement, as yoga was outlawed in the Soviet Union. His father was a greatly revered Russian poet, and I was taken to see a statue of him in Red Square. To my delight he took me to the Chekhov Museum and the Pushkin Museum of Fine Art. We also stood in a long queue in Pushkin Square in order to eat at the newly opened McDonald's, which of course wasn't my choice! I got to know and love Jacob and his family, and he kindly took me to the airport when I left.

I was tremendously moved by the amount of loving care I received at this time. Vera and Victor gave up their bedroom for me, a complete stranger. As a vegetarian, Vera stood in long queues after work to buy me vegetables for our meals. Food was particularly scarce during this time. I left Russia feeling that I had been nurtured and cared for in a way that was completely foreign to me, and was full of admiration for the strength of the Russian people I had the privilege of encountering. Determined to master the language, on my return home I began to attend a weekly Russian language course, which I continued for the next three years.

I spent that Christmas and the New Year of 1992 with yoga friends Tamara and James in their village in Spain. They had stayed with me over Christmas at my cottage in Gloucestershire, and also in Somerset. The highlight of my visit was a trip to Granada and the wonders of the Alhambra.

In March Melanie gave birth to twin boys, and I found

myself thrilled to be a grandma. I hadn't been ready to take on that role previously. My sights were always firmly on my work. This would be a new departure in my busy life, where I continued to run weekend workshops in body-orientated psychotherapy and Gestalt in London, yoga at Hawkwood, and neo-Reichian training at a centre near Exeter.

At the beginning of June I flew to Moscow for another international conference, and this time I was booked to run several neo-Reichian workshops with psychiatrists and psychologists. I found working with Russian participants very different from those in Britain. These were people who had grown up in a closed, restrictive and suspicious society, and here I was asking them to reveal their innermost thoughts, memories and feelings. Of course there was some resistance, and it was more important than ever for me to gain their trust. As academics, I suspect that working through the body, and the exercises I presented, was quite new to them, and I was impressed at the way they accepted my work, and enjoyed it. While there I managed to attend an exciting concert in Red Square, which went on into the early hours of the next morning, and on two successive evenings I was fortunate enough to watch the renowned Moscow Circus, and operettas by Mozart and Rossini. After ten days I left for Lithuania with Agni, a young woman I had met at the conference the previous year. We were to stay at her aunt's flat in Vilnius, from where I explored the city and visited a castle at Trakai. Although there must have been at least forty years between us, we became firm friends and had a great evening of dancing together the first night in her aunt's sitting room. The next day we left for Agni's home in Marijampolė, where we spent an enjoyable day with her mother and brother swimming and picnicking by a lake before our return to Vilnius.

I had arranged to travel on to St Petersburg. After a fourteen-and-a-half-hour train journey through Latvia and Estonia, I arrived at 1.30 in the morning, in broad daylight, to be met by Olga, an English-speaking Russian who was to be my hostess. During the next few days she was my guide in that beautiful city with its canals, reminding me of Amsterdam. Olga worked at the Russian Museum and was able to get me tickets to see its Russian art, and also to the magnificent Hermitage. One evening I was thrilled to attend a performance of contemporary ballet at the famous Mariinsky Theatre. I was able to visit Peter the Great's summer palace by boat, still being renovated after damage sustained during the war, and the fortress where he and subsequent Tsars are buried. The bones of Tsar Nicholas and his family, murdered by the Bolsheviks, had just been placed there after the recent discovery of their secret burial place in woods.

I was fortunate to be staying in a family flat where Olga's grandmother still lived. She described to me how her "babushka" had braved the minefields surrounding the city during the two-year siege of Leningrad, to pick whatever vegetation she could find outside the city walls to feed her family in the most dangerous conditions. There was simply no food available at all after a while, and many thousands of people froze or starved to death at that time. I had researched that period for the production I did of *The Promise* at Group 64 in the '70s, which dealt with the lives of three young people during that grim period of history. Before leaving home I had been asked by a meditation teacher I knew to look up a young couple, Oleg and Svetlana, who after introducing me to their Buddhist temple took me home with them for a meal, and next day showed me around the Alexander Nevsky Monastery.

On the overnight train back to Moscow I found myself in a compartment with three men sharing bottles of vodka, and thinking nothing of waking me up every few hours to offer me a glass! There was one day in Moscow before returning home when I took the metro to have tea with Jacob and his wife at their flat filled with precious heirlooms passed down through his family over generations. Once again I was deeply touched by the warmth of hospitality I received – a further demonstration of the Russian "soul". To my horror, arriving at the airport on my way home, I was informed that my visa had expired, and it was only after being marched to an office, where I was obliged to pay a hefty fine, that I was allowed to catch my plane.

Later that year, on returning from a workshop in Notting Hill Gate, I found myself being mugged by three young men. I managed to hang onto my handbag while they pushed me to the ground, and when I started to scream they ran off with only my scarf. After travelling the world without harm, it was ironic I should be attacked in that way on home ground!

At Easter 1993 I joined a group of teacher friends on a trip to Ireland. We arrived by ferry at Fishguard, and proceeded to drive through familiar-sounding names – Wexford, Waterford, Limerick and Tipperary – until we arrived at a remote cottage in Ballyvorn in Galway. It was a new experience for me to be on holiday with a group of women, and I still found myself loping off on my own during the next few days to explore the strangely mysterious ancient landscape with the soft light of this western region.

Return to Russia

At the beginning of September I returned to Moscow to run two weekend workshops arranged for me by my friend Vladimir. Unfortunately, on the train up to London, a new backpack, with all my course notes, including Russian translations for my students, and food and presents for my hosts, was stolen from the luggage rack. I was naturally extremely upset and wondered how I was going to manage. On arrival at the airport I was met by Vladimir and a young man named Vlad, and taken to stay with the Ivanova family, where I was offered tea and cake before bed. I hated having to arrive at their home empty-handed.

The morning of the first workshop I was collected by Vlad, and together with Galla, the family's daughter, and Peter, who was to be my interpreter (in spite of my Russian language lessons I was far from fluent enough to teach in the language), we were driven across Moscow, taking in the river, the parliamentary buildings of the White House, and the impressive monument to Yury Gagarin and the space projects. At our venue, a sanatorium for sick children, we worked till 6.30 that day and the next, with seventeen participants. Arriving back at eight o'clock I was offered a welcoming meal by Madam Ivanova, a large enthusiastic blonde lady who insisted on offering me cake for breakfast and dinner! During the week before the second workshop, when it rained continually, I was looked after by Vladimir and other members of the group. I was taken to visit the Tretyakov Museum, to see icon paintings, to the house of Stanislavsky, the famous theatre director, actor, teacher and co-founder of the Moscow Art Theatre, and to a memorable concert of a choral work with over a hundred choristers, and Tchaikovsky's Sixth Symphony at the Tchaikovsky Conservatoire Concert Hall. This was the composer played in a way I had never heard before, with a passion that only Russian musicians, who understand him, can express. I was deeply moved. Returning back one evening on a bus there was an incident involving two elderly women attempting to board the vehicle, when it pulled away suddenly, and one of the women fell back heavily onto the pavement. The bus stopped and I rushed to help, offering the shocked woman drops of rescue remedy I had in my handbag, while assuring her with the use of the word *bracht*, Russian for doctor! When we got off at the same stop, I offered her a long stemmed rose from the bouquet of roses I had been given by my students. This was one of several bouquets I received that always had an odd number of flowers, apparently a Russian custom. After the final workshop we partied with much singing, dancing and drinking. Then I somehow had enough energy to go on to an extraordinary production of Genet's *The Maids*, with an all-male cast in a wonderfully inventive scenic presentation.

I had arranged to stay on in Russia for another few days to visit Yaroslavl, currently twinned with Exeter. I had previously met Natasha at a gathering for cultural relations with Russia in Devon, and she had invited me to stay at her parental home there. I was not prepared for the bitterly cold weather in September, and spent a miserable time in that rather ugly town, feeling ill, with a heavy chest cold. Arriving back in Moscow, I was met with a farewell party at Ivanova's flat, plus new friends from my workshops, where they insisted on my drinking Russian brandy all evening.

On my return home to Totnes I found the front door jammed, preventing me from entering, and discovered my bedroom window had blown out during a storm! The next day I watched news on TV of the historic siege of the White House in Moscow that I had so recently travelled past each day!

I had been invited to return to Russia and teach the following year, 1994, and I suggested making it a winter visit with the romantic idea of experiencing Russia in thick snow, preferably at a country venue after my series of chest infections in the polluted air of Moscow. A date was set, but ten days before I became seriously ill with bronchitis, and it became apparent that it would be dangerous for me to consider travelling to Russia at this time. I had a great deal of difficulty in communicating with Vladimir, and when I finally reached him by telephone with a plea to find someone else to take the weekend workshop, his reply was "Never, it is you we want, Roslyn!" It appeared he not only had people booked to attend from different parts of Russia, but also some from America. Heaven knows why, Americans have excellent workshop leaders of their own! Of course they would be bringing much needed dollars. I felt terrible about letting them all down, but the fact remained that I was too ill to travel and run a workshop in sub-zero temperatures. I realised that this might be the end of my Russian working connection, for which I was saddened.

A highlight of that year was a visit to Findhorn for a ten-day workshop on conflict resolution with Arnie Mandel and his wife Annie from the United States, who had been working with traumatised people, victims of the war in the former Yugoslavia. I was interested in using the work in the new South Africa. With more than a hundred of us enacting the roles of victims and persecutors, including Jews and Nazis in Germany, it became an intensely emotional experience.

The year 1995 was the start of a complete decline in my health, which was eventually diagnosed as ME, or chronic fatigue syndrome. Halfway through January I caught Melanie's 'flu while she was staying with me, and

I was forced to cancel a flight to Johannesburg to stay with my friend Jo, and then another booking a couple of weeks later. This was the year that I had arranged a number of new workshops, including Scotland, London, and Greece. One by one I was forced to cancel the workshops as I remained feeling weak and ill. However I made a big effort to get to Israel for my mother's ninetieth birthday. After a birthday tea and dinner in Haifa, which I was unable to eat, I was taken to Jerusalem, the Dead Sea and En Gedi, and a kibbutz near Eilat, where my youngest niece lives with her American husband. In spite of feeling so ill, the visit was important in that I made an effort to get to know a little more of my mother's history by spending time with her. This would be my last opportunity, for the next time I saw her she was senile and semi-conscious with double pneumonia.

South Africa

At the end of October I had decided to spend three months in South Africa for the sake of my health and to view the new Rainbow Society with the possibility of returning to live in the country of my birth again. I began by spending three and a half weeks in Johannesburg, staying with Jo and then Norah, my old speech and drama teacher. Staying in Norah's house proved problematic. It was like living in a fortress. Interior as well as exterior doors had to be unlocked and locked again behind one. Escaping into the garden required the same procedure. Norah was beginning to show signs of senility with repetition of statements, and forgetting to turn off the gas on the cooker. Her driving was quite dangerous, such as failing to stop at red lights, and on one occasion while returning from a visit to her cousin, which she had been doing for many years, she missed the turning off for Johannesburg. Although I pointed it out she continued driving, refusing to believe that she could possibly be going the wrong way. She had always been such a strong, independent, highly respected woman, at one time recognised as South African Woman of the Year. It was sad for us both to witness her inevitable deterioration. However staying with Jo again and meeting her family made me happy. Apart from the constant fear of robbery and attack, white inhabitants still manage to live a charmed life.

My next stay was to be in Cape Town. I had arranged to be in a Salvation Army hotel in Fish Hoek, overlooking the beach in that small seaside town. A week later I had moved to a backpacker's hostel in Cape Town. After I had met up with Michael Wetzler, a doctor who had worked for some time at the Bristol Cancer Centre, now living in South Africa, he offered me accommodation in a hut in his garden, with the use of his kitchen. He had founded a holistic medical clinic recently, which I was interested to visit, and I spent a hot Sunday afternoon working in its new garden. Unfortunately I managed to set his microwave on fire, after setting a potato to cook for twenty minutes. I had had no previous experience with microwave machines. Soon after I had to move out as he was expecting family to stay!

My next accommodation was with a beauty specialist and her Afrikaans husband in a corrugated-roofed outhouse. They were vegetarians. I was charged £6 a day including meals, which consisted of an identical dish of unflavoured vegetables every day. Consequently I aimed to have as many meals out as I could afford. They kept a huge dangerous dog behind a gate in their house, which I dreaded having to meet. I attended midnight mass on

Christmas Eve held by Archbishop Desmond Tutu, who on looking round the congregation repeated the words "I love you, and you, and you," and one felt the love he was sending forth. What an inspiring man! As Christmas dinner chez the beauty specialist was to consist of a pizza her son was bringing round, I was relieved to be invited by a new friend, a Gestalt therapist, to a traditional sumptuous meal.

In the new year of 1986 I caught an overnight Translux coach in Cape Town one afternoon to Pietermaritzburg in KwaZulu-Natal, arriving early the next morning. I had booked to attend a couple of meditation retreats with Martine and Stephen Batchelor, at the Buddhist Retreat Centre in Ixopo. I knew them from Sharpham, a Buddhist community at that time, and Gaia House, a retreat centre, both situated near Totnes. An American woman, Kendal, had offered to drive me to the centre, after collecting me off the coach and taking me home with her for breakfast and a rest. Here is what I wrote about it on my return home—

The Buddhist Retreat Centre at Ixopo, like Yeats' words in his poem Innisfree, is a place where "peace comes dropping slow". Set in the lower foothills of the Drakensberg Mountains, often shrouded in mist, it exists in a quiet, timeless world of extraordinary beauty. An hour away from Pietermaritzburg it is finally arrived at by a couple of dirt roads through a wood of gum trees ending in parkland. Here, among rhododendron-lined pathways are hidden a thatched-roofed studio and meditation hall. Further down an incline can be found the kitchen, dining hall, office buildings and shop. In another area of the estate is the lodge, a long wooden building on a slope where visitors stay in simple individual cells leading off a central stepped corridor. Each cell looks out through a window from floor to ceiling to a tranquil view beyond. Several discreetly hidden dwellings house the white staff, and beyond the kitchen, the Zulu staff. All this is set in 125 hectares of lush parkland, indigenous forest and grassland. There is a walk to a dam and large lake, home to a wealth of wildlife, including nesting blue swallows. Two significant areas are the sites of the giant stone Buddha, as high as the nearby established trees, his gaze directed across lawns, paths and flowering bushes. The other is a Buddhist stupa reached along a path from the dining hall, past a pine wood, and ending on a high ridge overlooking one of the great valleys of the Umkomaas River. Viewed from this convenient outcrop of rocks is this surprisingly green and dramatic valley below leading upward to several hills beyond. Nestled in the folds of these hills can be seen Zulu villages of mud-walled thatched rondavels, from where the occasional sound of voices rises up. It is difficult to believe with this peaceful scene that, only a few years previously, violence had erupted in this valley, and on one occasion even threatened the retreat centre. The small town of Ixopo, whose inhabitants were almost entirely white, but now almost completely black, is some twenty minutes away. It is on the road to Ixopo that Alan Paton sets the opening lines of his book *Cry the Beloved Country*.

I was loath to leave this idyllic place, but I was to return on two more occasions in the years ahead. After spending a night at Kendal's home, I caught a Greyhound bus back to Johannesburg. The afternoon before Kendal took me to the University of Natal, where she lectured on drama. There I was introduced to Paul, responsible for dance movement, and we discussed the possibility of my running some workshops on movement for his department in the future. The fact that there was no money available at the time didn't look exactly hopeful. In Johannesburg there were three days in which to visit my uncle Oscar, the last of my father's four brothers, say goodbye to Norah, and Merilyn from my early theatre days, before flying back to London. The three months I had spent in South Africa confirmed for me that my hopes for change were premature. In fact very little had changed, apart from one important factor – black people I saw in urban areas had gained a new sense of themselves, a sense of dignity. People walked past me on the pavements instead of stepping off into the gutter to make way for me. They were beginning to throw off the colonial yoke in this new South Africa. However there was little evidence of change among the white inhabitants. It would need another generation to do that. Much of what had influenced me to leave the country initially was still part of everyday life. There was no way I would want to live in that environment again. I had to abandon my hope to do some conflict and resolution work with people there in the future. In any case it needed South Africans who had lived through the terrible days of Apartheid to take on that position.

I had let my house for six months, and with three months still to go I arranged to rent Marigold Cottage in Baltonsborough, near Glastonbury, belonging to Lesley, the old friend who had lent me some money to help buy Willow Cottage. I was now near enough to my family to help out with babysitting and be there for the twins' fourth birthday. I began to teach yoga locally, and joined a healing group.

Movement and Meditation

In October I began a form of movement with Helen Poyner that appeared to be an extension of the form of movement work I continued to use with my clients, and in my workshops and trainings. This was about allowing the body to move with its own energy, without the use of music to direct with rhythm and intention. Coming from a sense of personal truth, of integrity and authenticity, the body will move or not in its own way, with awareness, supported by feet or floor. This was the first of many experiences of working with her, first in Exeter, then in Dorset in a school hall, and on the beach among the rocks, or on the cliffs in rain, wind and sun.

In the spring of 1997 Namgyal Rinpoche began the first of his courses at the Orchard, a centre on the Welsh-Herefordshire borders run by a shiatsu trainer, Sonia Moriseau, and her partner, Ad Brugman. It was in a property next to the Orchard that the Crystal Group finally created their first centre in England. From a derelict cottage in four acres of land with a splendid view towards the Black Mountains, we have created a fine centre that can sleep several people in the house and several more in three huts in the grounds, with an added toilet and shower block. I have spent many memorable retreats there since.

That summer I was fortunate to meet the highly respected and pioneering Indonesian movement master, Suprapto, and to take part in a session he ran. This was the first of a number of other opportunities to work with him over a period of time on his visits to Europe. He created the Amerta Movement as a way of developing awareness, presence of body, mind and being, growing organically out of his background in Buddhism. About this time I joined a weekly movement peer group, consisting of other dance-movement teachers and people experienced in movement work, which I have continued to attend every Thursday morning ever since, whenever I am able, and it has continued to be a creative and nourishing part of my life in Totnes. Movers have come and gone through the years, but I seem to have remained with the group forever!

This was the year that I began regular body-work workshops for the Centre for Humanistic Psychology in Exeter, and the year I started creative writing classes culminating in a certificate in creative writing a few years on. The assessment then included writing in several genres, such as poetry, reportage, short story, radio play and diary keeping. In 1998 I enjoyed a writing holiday on the Greek island of Sími, where the group wrote at an ancient church, a museum and around the fascinating harbour.

For my seventieth birthday in January the following year I chose to visit Stratford-on-Avon for a production of Turgenev's *A Month in the Country*, which I had first seen as a teenager at the old Standard Theatre in Johannesburg, with Gwen Ffrangcon-Davies playing the principle part. Melanie drove us, and we spent a night at a hotel and met up with my old school friend, Marge, for a champagne dinner before the performance. It was probably the first time I had splashed out in such a way for my birthday, and where better than in the Bard's birthplace!

I had gone up to London that Easter to visit my old friend John Wiles, now sadly dying of cancer in a hospice in Wimbledon. He was unconscious during the two days I sat at his bedside, until on Easter Monday, on telling him my name while I held his hand, he lifted my hand to his lips, and died a few hours later. He meant a lot to me, as he did to Melanie. He had that ability to give one his total attention, as though there was no one more important than oneself at that moment. He had always been so interested in Melanie's work and mine, and I knew I would miss him dearly. I gave an address at the funeral in which I spoke of his many attributes and of our long friendship. At a ceremony following, made up of friends, some from the BBC, we sat in Quaker-type silence until one of those present felt moved to speak about him too, including an emotional daughter. Later a small group of us with raised umbrellas to protect us from the relentless rain came together among the dripping willows, to scatter his ashes with expectant ducks at Pen Ponds in his beloved Richmond Park, where a sudden playful gust of wind blew the ashes back at us!

That summer I flew to the south of France to teach yoga, movement and meditation at a holiday course centre for four weeks, among fields of sunflowers. It was there at the swimming pool that I viewed the solar eclipse. Although not complete, as in Britain, it was nevertheless awe-inspiring. What a way to finish the century!

Author, Melanie and the twins, Totnes, 1992

Boris and Jack Thompson Roylance (photo Paul Roylance)

PART SIX
2000–2010

The Writer and Eternal Student

Towards Freedom

Death of the Rinpoche

Change

If I could change the hearts
Of those who harbour thoughts
Of exploitation and deeds of destruction
Of nature's precious gifts,

If I could turn the minds of those
Who plan wars with no regard
For their fellow-man
And the suffering they cause,

If I could witness peoples of different faiths
Joining together in a common bond
To sing and dance and laugh together
With acceptance with love and respect
Seeing the other as reflection of themselves

I should die happy.

This was the era of the invasions and war in Afghanistan and Iraq, when I joined a peace group in Totnes. Over a period of several years we held a peace vigil for an hour every Saturday morning, holding banners of protest outside the fine, local, red Devonian sandstone church of St Mary, led by a wonderful elderly couple, Lillian and Donald Brown. The poem was written during that time.

This last decade highlights my significant meditation retreats, my continued involvement with dance movement, and my developing interest in green environmental and peace issues, by taking part in vigils, protests against GM foods, and championing the Occupy Movement. The establishment of Transition Town Totnes by Rob Hopkins has been a particular joy for me and I have endeavoured to be involved where I could in community projects. It has been heartening to witness the spread of transition towns through so many other countries in the world, a sign of the growing need for people to find alternative solutions to our exploitative, materialistic, commercial societies in the West.

Here are my memorable events of this decade, consisting largely of meditation retreats. In 2000 I spent five days in southern France at a retreat in a field of marquees with the Dalai Lama and 12,000 others, swelling to 14,000 at the weekend! The opening day was eventful for the arrival of a cloudburst of torrential rain, which completely flooded the large presenting marquee, making it impossible to start the retreat until the following day.

In September 2003 the Rinpoche arrived at Maitreya House to bless this our new meditation centre in Herefordshire, and to give a wonderful dzogchen retreat on emptiness, during which the students were instructed to lie out one night under the stars for a certain time, with arms and legs spread, star bathing. On the night in question the sky cleared from its blanket of clouds and revealed a magnificent display of twinkling lights! This course was a particularly profound experience, and without our knowing it the last we were ever to receive from him. Three weeks later, after teaching in Germany and Switzerland, the Rinpoche was dead. Apparently his energy had been deteriorating during his teaching in Europe, and at the end of the course in Switzerland, staying at a student's house on Lake Constance, he spoke of a pain in his chest, and soon after quietly slipped away. I would like to have gone immediately to Switzerland, together with a few of his students, to be able to sit with his body laid out in state for a couple of days, which the authorities authorised before the cremation. However I was booked to leave a few days later for Canada, arranged some weeks before, after it had been suggested that I attend a ceremony connected to my yidam (individual mantra) that the Rinpoche was planning to give at the Dharma Centre of Canada. After thirty years, I was once again to travel to the centre for a teaching from him, and he would not be there! I felt completely overwhelmed during those intense days. He had been so much part of my life for the last thirty years! It was difficult to believe that he was no more.

A late photograph of the Rinpoche, 2003, six weeks before his death in Switzerland, after blessing Maitreya House in Herefordshire

Canada

I travelled to Toronto at the same time as the Rinpoche's ashes were being brought from Switzerland by Terry, his attendant. What followed at the centre was the most amazing gathering of students from all over the world, to celebrate the life of a great teacher. I was so glad to be there among others whose lives had also been changed by this extraordinary man. What an emotional experience! In a giant marquee beside the house, we were able to experience a résumé of Rinpoche's life through photos, and film, and many students' account of their time with him. I also spoke a few words at the microphone, and joined with several hundred others in a line to lay a garland on a shrine built to house his ashes. A few days later, Sonam, his earliest British student from the 1960s, gave me the empowerment I had come to receive, in the temple with a number of others attending. These empowerments are linked to various Tibetan deities with their accompanying mantras. After attending an empowerment or wong kur one is expected to do 100,000 mantras over a period of time, counting on a mala or rosary. This I have done with a few of the many empowerments in which I have participated. The vibration of the mantra will have a particular, sometimes quite powerful effect. I have always loved the ritual of these ceremonies encompassing sound, colour and symbolism.

The following year there was a retreat with the young Seventeenth Karmapa – Trinley Thaye Dorje – in France. I had taken refuge with his predecessor, the Sixteenth Karmapa in London in 1978. The Karmapa, as head of the Karma Kagyu section of Tibetan Buddhism, is equivalent in importance in the Tibetan tradition to the Dalai Lama. At the end of that year I left for New Zealand for one of the most momentous periods of my life.

New Zealand

Before leaving for New Zealand I visited my doctor, who after sounding my pulse, warned me that if I found myself feeling faint and sick, I was to visit a doctor. So it transpired that two weeks after arriving in Auckland, still suffering as I thought from jetlag, and having stayed at Waiheke Island for a week, I travelled north to the Bay of Islands to visit a friend of a friend. On the morning of my second day there, I woke feeling dizzy and sick. I asked to see a doctor, who on examining me wrote a letter for a local hospital. After a series of tests there I was transported by ambulance the same day to a bigger hospital in Whangarei, some distance away, where I remained for the next six days. When the Chinese consultant informed me that I would be having a pacemaker implantation, and I questioned the decision with "What if I refuse?" his reply was "Well, your heart might just stop, so you have no choice, have you?" Although I don't like being given orders, this conversation stopped me in my tracks. On 22nd December I was transferred to Auckland City Hospital, and operated on the next afternoon. Discharged on Christmas Eve I was so thankful and relieved to have the perfect place and situation in which to recuperate. Before leaving home I had booked to spend Christmas and New Year at Tauhara, a New Age centre on Lake Taupo in the centre of the North Island. I was collected from the hospital and driven to this perfect refuge by another visitor. There I was lovingly looked after and given healing and excellent food. On the 29th December, while making a phone call to friends in Wellington, where I was planning to stay next, I found an old newspaper in the phone booth that was full of news of the catastrophic tsunami that had struck on Boxing Day. What an eventful period this was proving to be!

In Wellington I stayed with Cashy, who I hadn't seen for twenty years. She had been chairperson of the Crystal Group and another of my lodgers in Putney. It was so good to see her again and meet her lovely daughters, and continue to be taken care of. Then on to Nelson in the South Island, staying with Keith, also formerly of the Crystal Group, and meeting after twenty years. From there I explored the South Island by bus staying in backpacker accommodation. The highlight of this time was a helicopter ride to the top of Franz Josef and Fox Glaciers, where I did a dance in the snow. Another expedition after returning to Nelson was not so pleasant. On a visit to Abel Tasman National Park I chose a speedboat trip to the northern point of Tasman Bay, with the idea of a scenic walk along the coast to Torrent Bay, to be collected there later that day. The weather wasn't good when we set out, and I questioned whether to go at all, but since I and the friend I was with had already booked the day before, and didn't want to lose our money, we continued with the trip. Meanwhile the weather deteriorated. The walk proved to be a nightmare. The rain soon became torrential with nowhere to shelter. All we could do was keep going until we reached the arranged meeting point for the boat to pick us up. When we finally arrived there, soaked to the skin, and after about an hour's wait on the beach with no shelter, the boat appeared but was unable to land, because of the rough sea. The crew signalled for us and a few others waiting, to wade out to the boat. As the oldest and slowest I was the last on board in a violently rocking journey back to base, being further soaked by spray!

A week later I was on my way to the Wangapeka Dharma Study and Meditation Retreat. This was my *raison d'être* for visiting New Zealand. Tarchin Hern, co-founder of the centre, had shown me photos of the place a year or two before at Maitraya House, on a visit there to give a retreat, and invited me to attend a six-month study course starting in March 2004. As I had already used up three months of my six months' visa, I would be able to do only the first three months of the course. They proved to be one of the happiest and fulfilling times of my life! As an early student and attendant of the Rinpoche, which was when I first knew him, Tarchin's teachings are greatly influenced by his teacher and also those of Thich Nhat Hanh, the Vietnamese teacher. The days were filled with courses on biology, examining micro-organisms under powerful microscopes, astronomy, with the use of equally powerful telescopes, study of the body and in particular the brain, exercises to develop the senses, and Feldenkrais practice, delivered by some visiting teachers. Each day there would be a morning puja and evening meditation session, and at other times sitting and walking meditation. The latter was a particularly beautiful experience, walking slowly through the forest area that rose up behind the centre. Here were wild pigs to watch out for that dug up the paths, and as autumn progressed the most magnificent orange and yellow toadstools and mushrooms appeared. The centre was set in 600 acres of hill forest, land flanked on one side by a mountain named Jones Ridge and facing, far below, the magnificent winding Wangapeka River. Some mornings walking up hill on the way to the meditation room before breakfast, the view was obscured by a mist of cloud below, while we remained above in the clear air. Here are a couple of poems I wrote at that time.

Silent Walking

Ever so slowly, one foot placed in front of the other,
the forest leaves and fallen needles so soft
beneath the feet as we snake our way
through tracks of fern and majestic pine

our eyes on the path, hands folded, spines erect.

Matching the steps to my breath, while today
I contemplate the wonder of impermanence;
hoping that next time we stop I will land
on a sunny spot, in the early morning chill,
and to make sure when we do,
I take an extra step or two.

What plans I hatch as I walk, what things I will do,
my body responds with tingles of joy.
Reluctantly bringing my mind back to breathing
I notice, just too late, that the person in front
has suddenly stopped!

Dawn at Wangapeka

My heart fit to burst at the sight of the sky
streaks of orange and purple, then gold,
with shy pink clouds like candyfloss
adding to the music,
what an orchestra of sound!

Meanwhile across the gully
there looms Jones Ridge in shadow
imposing and hugely present,
while rabbits sit and ponder,

bounce away, or chase each other
over ever brightening patches of turf.
And oh, the birds, the joyous sound
of the tui, or is it the bellbird
which imitates the tui?
Of course we will never know.
Now leaves are blowing in a cloud
a shower of red and gold.

What bliss it is to be here
in the wind, the rain and the sun
whose warmth creeps in my very bones
enabling me to let go.
There is nowhere else I would rather be
than here – right now.

Reluctantly the time came for me to leave. I felt renewed
– quite blissful. What a joyous time this had been!
Travelling back to Auckland I stopped at Rotorua, for a
few days, with its hot springs and Maori culture, and a
brief visit to two New Age centres in the Coromandel
Peninsula in the north of the island, where I ran a dance
workshop. I had managed to offer two dance workshops
while I was at the Wangapeka Centre. A memorable
event at the centre had been the scattering of some of
Rinpoche's ashes together with rose petals, into the
Wangapeka River – ashes brought by Terry from Canada,
watched by about sixty of his New Zealand students. I

helped to cook a main meal for them all that day, when I managed to overestimate the amount of food needed, and ended up serving our course-group ratatouille for the next two days!

Before leaving New Zealand I found I had seen the inside of five hospitals, being obliged to visit for check-ups every few weeks, wherever I was staying.

Tarchin's scattering of Rinpoche's ashes.
Wangapeka River, 2005

Conclusion

In the next few years, back home, I took a diploma course in creative writing and wrote a number of poems in a weekly poetry class, sometimes reading them in public. It had been suggested to me by a friend that at this stage of my life I should consider being less active and think about beginning to write, which struck a chord. However I continued to practise tai chi and qigong, including a course in Italy; continued with my weekly peer movement group, and courses with the remarkable Javanese master Suprapto. I attended a heart-and-soul fortnightly group for two and a half years as part of Transition Totnes, and made two more visits to South Africa on meditation retreats, the second one being part of a Woza Moya Project, a work retreat in Kwa-Zulu Natal helping families with HIV/AIDS in a rural area near the Buddhist Centre, to create vegetable gardens to improve their health.

In 2009, shortly after my eightieth birthday, I was running round the large hall our movement group used each week. When, on deciding mid-flight that I would run the other way, to my surprise I found myself crashing to the floor. I had foolishly kept my socks on and slipped, with disastrous results. The heavy fall and fractured elbow was the start of a marked deterioration in my health. It didn't help my condition when, that autumn, on giving Melanie and the grandsons a treat of four days in Venice, I managed to fall out of the narrow iron bedstead in which I was sleeping on the last night, resulting in headaches and pressure in the head for the next couple of years. This was followed, eighteen months later, by a fall, while rushing up some ancient steep stone steps on the banks of the Nile, and fracturing my upper arm where it meets the shoulder. I had gone to Egypt to escape from the English winter and the chest infections I was prone to, but I was too late. By the time I reached the hotel on an island in the River Nile opposite Aswan, at the beginning of January, I was already infected, and spent four weeks feeling ill, until leaving, with some difficulty, a couple of days after the start of the Egyptian Revolution!

On recollecting my life as a psychotherapist, although there were many satisfactory outcomes of the psychotherapeutic process, I was reminded of a few episodes that sit uneasily in my memory. There was a young German boy during a workshop in Hanover among twenty-six students, who after delving into a deep state of consciousness on the first day failed to return on the following day. I was disturbed and unhappy at being unable to follow up his process to help him. Then there was the middle-aged man whose wife had followed a guru to America. He was devastated, as he saw it as a repeat of his mother's actions in abandoning him as a child. Sometime into his therapy, I was unable to see him one week, as I was booked on a dance course in Bristol. To my horror, on returning, I learned that he had taken his life while I was away. Experiencing me as abandoning him also was probably more than he could bear. Of course I felt I had let him down, and was full of remorse. It didn't really help to learn later from his daughter that he had attempted suicide on more than one occasion previously.

In summing up my life I am aware that although it has been a hard lonely journey, I have been blessed with a feeling of deep inner connection, the seeds of which I have to thank my father for, given his strong belief in divine healing through Christian Science, which he passed on to me. Of course I found my own spiritual path, but connecting to that healing energy has been an integral part of my lifework, whether through yoga, dance, complementary medicine or therapy. I do have some regrets for missed opportunities at certain times (too many to mention), when I lacked the confidence to grab them. I largely lost confidence in myself when Michael died in 1959, and I no longer had access to the encouragement and belief in myself that he offered me. I wonder how much more I might have achieved with the continued support of such a partner. I am also paradoxically aware of a certain arrogance which has prevented me from offering my experience when I could, and then wondering why I have felt undervalued! However, there is a sense of fulfilment in the knowledge that I always encouraged students, clients and workshop participants to develop their own unique potential. I have a firm conviction that with enough belief and perseverance in following one's passion, we can aspire to and achieve almost anything. In spite of it, although largely being a lone one, my life has given me the freedom to be creative in different ways, to take risks and venture into new and unknown territory. A great love in my life has been music, also nurtured by my father, who was in the possession of a fine dramatic tenor voice, and who instilled in me his love of classical music and opera. I had four different surnames at different periods of my life, but the one I chose myself as a stage name, Langdon, the name under which my father sang, was the one I felt belonged to me.

Now in my eighties, I am feeling the effects of aging, and realise how much I have had to slow down, which has given me the time to listen to more music, to study, read and meditate. Looking back on my work through the years, I have been struck by my preoccupation with the breathing process. In teaching voice production, yoga, in Reichian breath work, and in Buddhist meditation, work with the breath is essential. Has this preoccupation been a result of being born with the cord round my neck? In one of the primal sessions with the therapist David

Boadella, involving my birth, I was seen to breathe out, while failing to inhale again for at least thirty seconds, much to the consternations of my fellow-students.

I want to acknowledge my gratitude for the invaluable richness of the dharma teachings I have received through the years, which has informed my life. I am also grateful for the loving kindness and care I have received during these latter years from members of the local Quakers, and from members of my women's group. I am so thankful to have my daughter Melanie in my life, my greatest friend, and the enormous pleasure of my talented grandsons Boris and Jack, who have grown up to be friendly, loving human beings, with the prospect of becoming highly regarded filmmakers. I am also grateful for the guardian angel, or guiding force I have experienced from childhood, and which I feel has played such a large part in protecting me during my travels. I have always been my own person, setting my own standards and following my own set of rules and ethics. I have enjoyed setting myself challenges and have believed in taking calculated risks, at times as a part of living on the edge. I believe that my largely unconscious reason for opening this window on my life, by writing this work, has been to find the acceptance and appreciation that I wanted from my parents as a child and never received, and that I looked for as an actress and workshop facilitator. I experienced a taste of it as the four-year-old Sleeping Beauty, and have looked for it ever since. Perhaps on finally beginning to wake up I realise I don't need others to value me, I can appreciate myself. The Buddha described himself as a finger pointing to the moon. I like to think that at times during my life I was able to provide a sign to a small bridge leading across the river of life's sufferings, along the path leading to that finger. It has been a lonely, but richly rewarding journey, and I am not done yet. I now await the next adventure!

OM MANI PADME HUM

Jack and Boris, aged twenty-one

Lightning Source UK Ltd.
Milton Keynes UK
UKOW06f0022290815

257694UK00009B/102/P